D0070104

Children who are fortified with the social graces are considerate of others, are more apt to be self-assured, and able to cope in a variety of social settings.

When well-mannered children grow into self-controlled adults, they will find that polite behavior is a real plus whether they are looking for a job, dealing with difficult people, or coping with long lines at the grocery store.

Manners are practical, sensible, and believe it or not, they can and should be fun!

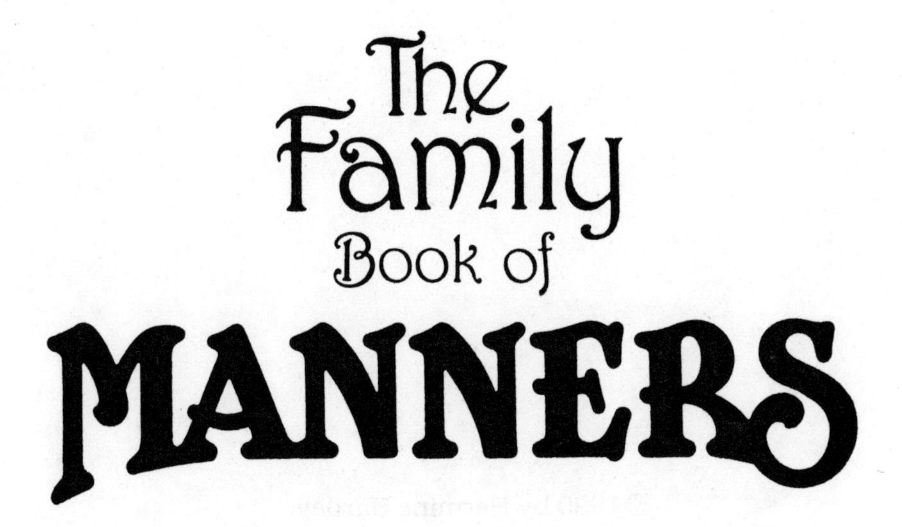


by

Hermine Hartley

Illustrated by Al Hartley

Barbour Books
Westwood, New Jersey

© 1990 by Hermine Hartley

ISBN 1-55748-151-2 - Hardbound
ISBN 1-55748-152-0 - Softbound

All rights reserved. No part of this publication may be reproduced or transmitted in any form or by any means without written permission of the publisher.

EVANGELICAL CHRISTIAN PUBLISHERS ASSOCIATION ecpa MEMBER

Published by: **BARBOUR AND COMPANY, INC.**
**P.O. Box 1219**
**Westwood, New Jersey 07675**

**Typesetting by: Typetronix, Inc., Cape Coral, FL**
**Printed in the United States of America**

I dedicate this book in love to
my children and grandchildren.

| <u>Alana</u> | <u>Fred</u> |
| --- | --- |
| John | Fred |
| Lee | Andrea |
| | Stephen |
| | Andrew |

# Contents

# INTRODUCTION

Welcome to the world of manners!

The more we know about manners, the better we'll feel . . . about ourselves and others.

Manners are more than using the right fork. They're using the right attitude. Our behavior can affect our relationships much more than our etiquette.

This book helps us to see that manners are not stuffy rules wearing white ties and tails. They can show up in sports shirts and jeans. The more they're seen, the more we're able to enjoy confidence instead of confusion and embarrassment.

Manners are to people what polish is to silver. Manners make us shine.*

---

* ***Shine as stars in the universe.***

*(see Philippians 2:15)*

---

# Good Manners Are for the Whole Family!

We can all take hold of the Golden Rule:

*"Do to others as you would like them to do to you."* (see Luke 6:31)

***"It's good to commit the Golden Rule to memory. It's better to commit it to life."***

*Ed Markham*

**This book is about what manners are all about.**

# The Dictionary sheds light on manners.

**Manners:** Socially correct behavior.
**Etiquette:** Conventional rules for correct behavior.
**Polite:** Good manners and tactful behavior.

Manners are simply a matter of how we behave. How we treat one another. Good manners show respect and consideration for others. They're not simply a veneer we put on. They come from the heart.

Good manners are really a form of love;

***"Love is patient, love is kind. It does not envy, it does not boast, it is not proud. It is not rude, it is not selfish, it is not easily angered, it keeps no record of wrongs."***

*1 Corinthians 13:4, 5*

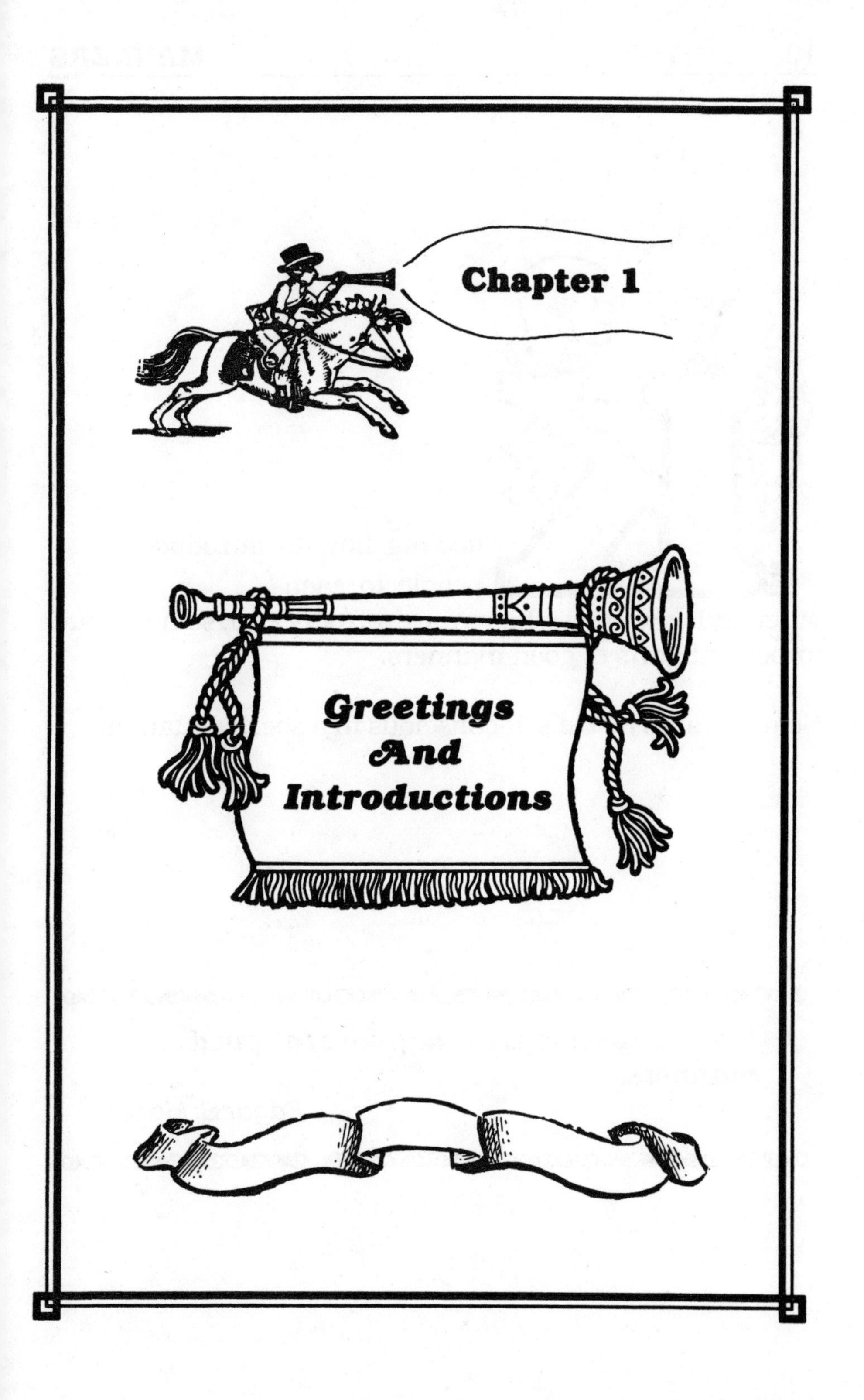
Chapter 1
Greetings
And
Introductions

Knowing how to introduce people to each other and how to act when we are introduced to someone are important parts of good manners.

No one wants to feel self-conscious in a social situation.

***"Self-respect is at the bottom of all good manners."***

*Edgar S. Martin*

We should always keep in mind that first impressions are often lasting impressions.

We want to be remembered as:

not as:

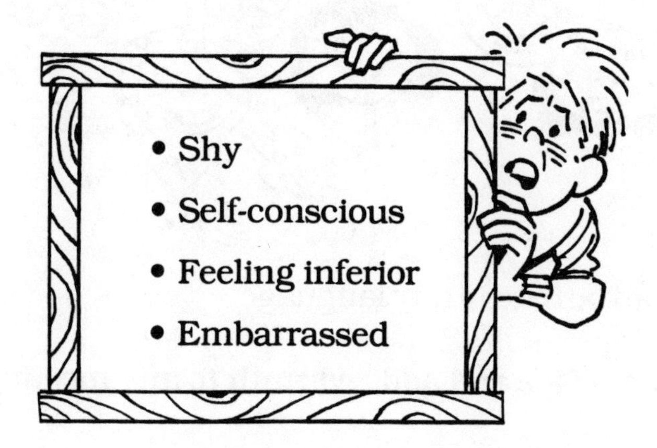


Good manners bring out the best in us.

## People are important

When we meet new people we want to let them know they are special to us.

We always want to:

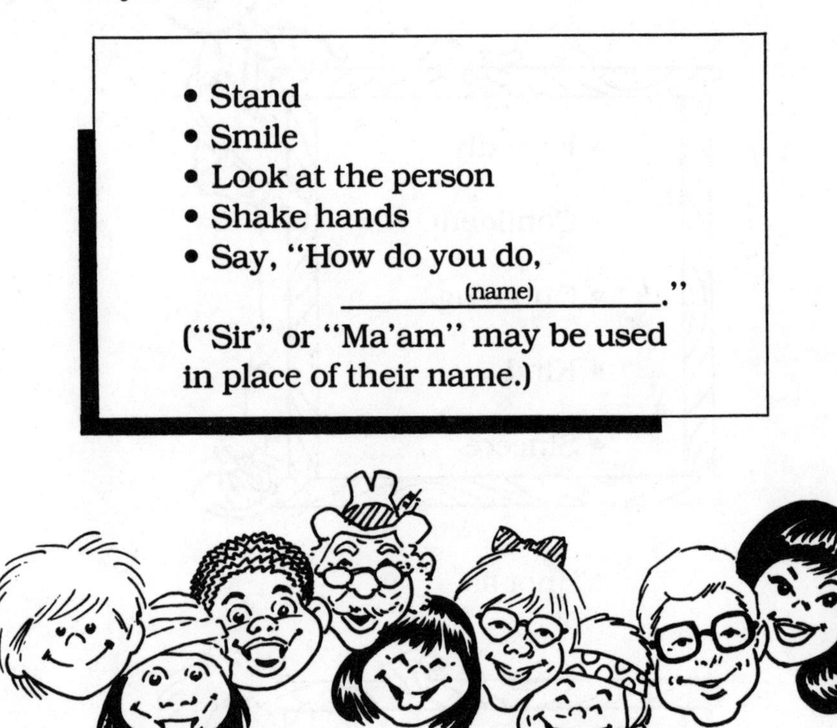

- Stand
- Smile
- Look at the person
- Shake hands
- Say, "How do you do, ______(name)______."

("Sir" or "Ma'am" may be used in place of their name.)

A smile can be read in any language.

It lights up a face and adds warmth to any meeting.

Smiles that come from the heart are the best kind. When you give one, you usually get one in return.

# HOW TO INTRODUCE PEOPLE

Always introduce a young person to an older one.

"Grandma, this is John Wilson. John, this is my Grandmother, Mrs. Jones."

Always introduce a man to a woman.

This shows special honor and respect to those of greater age as well as to women and girls.

Always introduce a boy to a girl.

"Sally, this is Joe, the captain of our football team."

If the person you are introducing has a title, be sure to use it as a sign of respect. Whenever possible, add something about the person you are introducing. "Dr. Smith is my dentist."

Often introductions take place in large groups amid some confusion and it can be difficult to remember names. Trying to also remember the rules of introductions might add too much to the general confusion. In such circumstances simply concentrate on saying all names loud and clear. That's the important part of any introduction.

When we leave someone we have just met, it is thoughtful to say something such as: "It was nice to meet you ____(say name)____."

***"Good manners is the art of making people comfortable in our presence. The one who makes the fewest people uneasy, has the best manners."***

*Jonathan Swift*

# HOW TO INTRODUCE YOURSELF

Sometimes there is no one around to introduce us to others.

We shouldn't be shy.

It's perfectly correct to introduce ourself by simply saying, "Hello, I'm Mary Brown."

# INTRODUCING A GROUP

When a group is small, we can usually introduce each person individually as they arrive, but as the group gets bigger, it gets more difficult. It becomes easier to say, "Friends, I'd like you to meet Peter Green. Pete, this is . . ." (indicate individual people as we mention each name).

Once the group becomes too large for this, or if someone arrives late, we simply say, "Friends, this is Peter Green. Please introduce yourselves to him."

# GREETINGS

A greeting should be warm and sincere.

"Betty! It's so good to see you!"

No one really enjoys being greeted by a limpid, "Hi" or a garbled, "humyghm."

The natural time to start to greet folks with enthusiasm is at breakfast with our own family. We tend to take cereal for granted, but we never want to do that to our family.

"Good morning, Mom.
I hope you're feeling great."

"I hope you had a good night's sleep, Dad."

Give everybody a kiss!

It'll give everyone a super start on the day!

**NOTE:**
Breakfast isn't much fun if everyone acts as though they resent being out of bed. Manners make every part of the day better. They add a lot more to the breakfast experience than oat bran.

When we greet someone we want to say more than just "Hi." It is better to say, "How are you?" Better yet, we should use their names: "Hello, Mrs. Lyle. I know your son Corkey from school." This gives Mrs. Lyle a clue as to who we are and helps her to start a conversation.

We should always greet people who enter the room we're in, even if we're busy at the time. If it's an adult, a relative, or someone from outside our family, it's always polite to stand up as they enter the room.

We never call an adult by their first name unless we've been given permission.

Of course, greeting always goes best when we do it cheerfully and with a pleasant smile on our face. We want our manners to be seen as a very natural part of our life-style.

Sometimes we will meet someone we haven't seen for a long time. We may not remember them, and they may not remember us.

This could be an awkward situation.

When this happens, we just say, "Hello, I'm Jane Brown. It's nice to see you again."

It's best not to say, "Remember me?" If they don't remember us, our question would place them in an embarrassing position.

Good manners are always considerate.

They release tension.

# SHAKING HANDS

- Men shake hands with each other when being introduced.
- Men shake hands with a woman if she extends her hand.
- Women shake hands with each other if they choose.
- We always use a firm handshake. Not too strong. Not too limp.

# *Summary*

People are special.

We never know how special the new folks we meet really are until we get to know them.

Getting through the introduction gracefully and enthusiastically helps us to convey the fact that we're truly "Glad to meet you."

Remember to:

* Smile sincerely
* Look directly at person
* Shake hands firmly
* Use their name
* Be friendly
* Enjoy the conversation

Chapter 2
Personal Manners

# Personal Manners

Each of us is a "Designer Edition." God doesn't use a cookie cutter. He made each of us to be

*"One of a kind!"*

We're special to Him!

He gave each of us a special body, special talents, and a special reason to enjoy the great adventure of life!

***"When God made us, He put the right wrapper around the right contents;***

***He put the right frame around the right picture.***

***He put the right body around the right spirit."***

*From the book FLOPS*
*by Fred A. Hartley, III*

Good manners always show appreciation. We want to show we're grateful for the gift of life.

# Our Bodies

Our bodies are an absolute miracle. No one will ever build a computer to equal the human brain. No pump will ever match the human heart. No camera or lens can equal the human eye. Our bodies are truly works of art. . . .

Because they are so special, we need to treat them with dignity and respect . . . don't abuse them. Take care of them.

* *Private parts of our bodies are exactly that . . .* ***private!***

* *Dirty jokes or stories about private parts of our bodies are an insult to our Creator.*

God isn't a prude but He wants us to be modest. Some folks will ridicule modesty. The real point is that God will applaud it.

* 1 Corinthians 13:6-8

# Taking Care of the Body We Live In

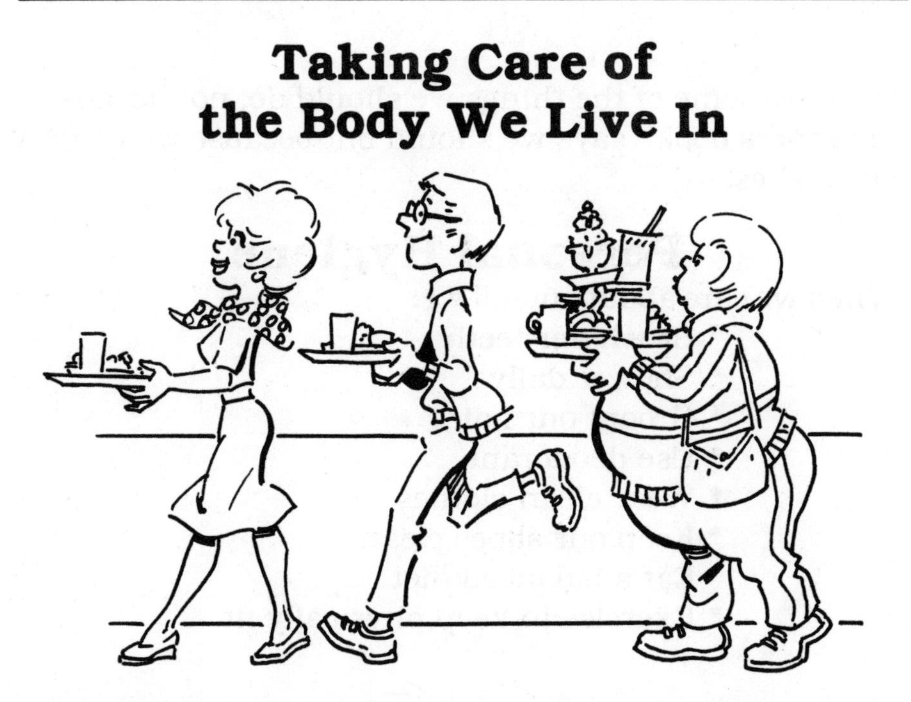

What we put into our bodies is important. Healthy food, healthy body, or as the computer people say, "Garbage in, garbage out." We are what we eat . . . and who wants to be junk food?

| **Good Food** | **Bad Food** |
|---|---|
| Fresh Fruit | Fried Foods |
| Vegetables | Sweets |
| Salads | Sodas |
| Whole Grain Breads | Bagged Snacks |
| Fish | Fats |
| Water | Caffeine Drinks |
| Complex Carbohydrates | Other "Junk Food" |

***"Dieters try to dispose of their hazardous waist."***

Here are some of the things we should do, not because a "manners book" says we should but because we respect our bodies!

## Personal Hygiene

When we care about ourself we:

* Brush our teeth
* Shower daily
* Groom our hair
* Use deodorant
* Wear clean clothes
* Keep our shoes clean
* Eat a balanced diet
* Exercise to keep physically fit.

Taking care of the bodies we live in pays off in very practical ways:

* Good health
* Good days
* Good friends

Did you ever notice that you stand taller when you feel good than when you feel bad?

There's more zip in your walk when you feel good; your attitude is better and there's more confidence in your voice.

By controlling our body posture, we control our mental outlook.

| **Weak Posture** | **Strong Posture** |
| --- | --- |
| Weakens self-esteem | Requires discipline |
| Impairs speaking ability | Influences better mental outlook |
| Fosters disrespect | Adds to our appearance |
| Invites failure | Suggests we have it all together |
| Decreases height | Suggests strength |
| Turns off opposite sex | Enhances our appearance |
| Shows weakness | Helps our clothes to fit better |
| Detracts strength | Helps us to speak better |
| Gives a bad impression | Increases lung capacity |
| Gives sense of dejection | Increases height |

***Good health comes from a strong* MORAL *posture, too!***

# My Values

IT MAKES A BIG DIFFERENCE
HOW WE **LOOK** AT THINGS
AND THE THINGS WE LOOK AT.

As important as it is to be clean on the outside, it's more important to be clean on the inside.

We all know that pollution is a real problem in the world today. Pollution is also a growing problem in many lives. There are habits and activities that can scar and destroy our lives along with air pollutants and chemical substances.

Avoiding this kind of personal danger is not always easy. Some friends, TV, and movies can make harmful things seem exciting, yet we all have a built-in alarm system . . . we call it conscience. A small buzzer alerts us to things that are bad for us. But we also have the freedom to ignore the alarm if we choose.

***"Out of men's hearts come evil thoughts, sexual immorality, theft, murder, adultery, greed, malice, deceit, lewdness, envy, slander, arrogance and folly. All these things come from inside and make a man 'unclean.' "***

*Mark 7:21-23*

## Danger signs

- X-rated movies
- Drugs
- Mind-altering substances
- Nicotine
- Pornographic magazines
- Dirty jokes
- Harmful habits

*"No one ever became very wicked all at once."*

***"The ladder of life is full of splinters that we don't feel until we backslide."***

# How Can I Help Myself?

**See No Evil** **Hear No Evil** **Speak No Evil**

- ★ Ask, "Would I like my parents to see me now?"
- ★ Be willing to say "no," even if everyone else is doing it.
- ★ Respect your sexuality and others'.
- ★ Choose your friends carefully.
- ★ Establish high standards for yourself.
- ★ Keep an open family communication and discuss things questionable.
- ★ Tell the truth.

> ***"No temptation has seized you except what is common to man. And God is faithful; He will not let you be tempted beyond what you can bear. But when you are tempted, He will also provide a way out so that you can stand up under it."***
>
> *1 Corinthians 10:13*

# Our Friends

More important than choosing the right fork is choosing the right friend.

Some friends can help us.
**Some friends can hurt us.**

We all need friends. Friends are important people in our lives. We tend to go along with friends, to do what they want to do, to protect them. All this is good **if our friends are good!** If they aren't, we find ourselves protecting someone who's wrong, doing wrong things, and we turn into the wrong kind of people ourselves.

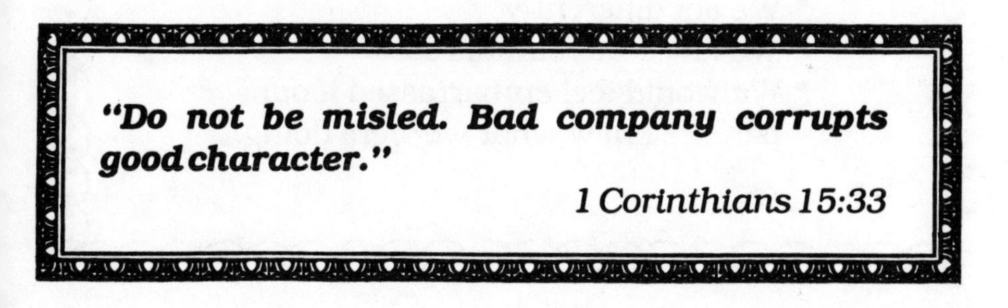

***"Do not be misled. Bad company corrupts good character."***

*1 Corinthians 15:33*

It really doesn't matter how good our manners are if our life's all wrong, does it? We may be polite and proper on the surface, but what we **do** says more about us than what we **say.**

We can get stuck and hurt far worse with the wrong friend than the wrong fork.

We must ask ourself . . .

* Do we have the same values?
* Do they do things our parents would disapprove of ?

We also need to understand there are true friends and there are false friends.

**With true friends**

* We can be honest
* We can be ourselves
* We can hold to our convictions
* We will never be ashamed.

**With false friends**

* We tell lies
* We act differently
* We lower our standards
* We would feel embarrassed if our parents knew what we were doing.

## To Be A Friend
*(The Ten B's)*

* **Be** sincere
* **Be** compassionate
* **Be** understanding
* **Be** considerate
* **Be** kind
* **Be** supportive
* **Be** honest
* **Be** courteous
* **Be** strong in your moral convictions
* **Be** trusting

***If we want to have a good friend, we need to be a good friend.***

## Tips for friendship

*"You can make more friends in two months by being interested in other people than you can in two years by trying to get other people interested in you."*

Dale Carnegie

***"My best friend is the one who brings out the best in me."***

**Henry Ford**

*"A friend is one who does their knocking before they enter instead of after they leave."*

Irene Keepin

***"It's better to keep a friend from falling than to help them up."***

**Arnold Glassow**

*"He who casts a friend aside like an old shoe is a heel without a soul."*

Parin

***"Our friends show us what we can do; our enemies teach us what we must do."***

**Goethe**

*"There are certain friends we can depend on. They're always around when they need us."*

Anonymous

There are all kinds of friendships for all kinds of reasons. True friends are loyal. They help us when we're down, celebrate with us when we're up. True friends give each other freedom.

We all have the freedom to end any friendship that is not healthy.

## Our Room

Our room is where we spend important time by ourselves. It's our special private place, for fun, for friends, for sleep, study, for many, many uses.

Our room tells more about us than our mirror. Are we neat or raunchy?

Do we care what kind of impression we make? Are our lives in order? Or in disorder?

**When a guest enters our room . . .**

* Can they see the furniture?
* Can they walk without tripping?
* Are our clothes hung up?
* Is our dresser neat?
* Is the bed made neatly?

We want our friends to think we're "neat." Our room is a good place to start. Why not surprise our parents today!

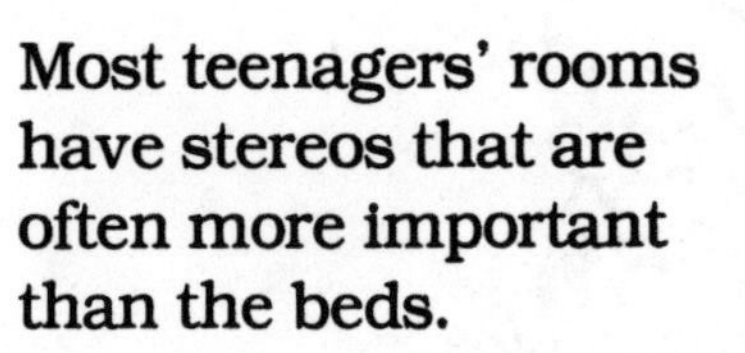

Most teenagers' rooms have stereos that are often more important than the beds.

It's a nice display of manners to make the volume level as comfortable as the bed. Someone in the next room may be trying to read. In extreme cases, someone on the next block may be trying to concentrate.

# Summary

- Our body — Stays healthy when treated properly. Meant to be clean on the inside as well as the outside.
- Our values — Critical to our life and our families, effect society.
- Our friends — Must be chosen carefully. They can help us or they can hurt us.
- Our rooms — Can reflect something about us. "The way you make your bed is the way you lie in it!"

## Chapter 3

# Table Manners And Dinner Parties

# Dinner Party Invitations

Whether a dinner invitation arrives by mail or telephone, a prompt reply is always considerate.

Formal written invitations may say "RSVP," an abbreviation for the French words for *Reply if You Please.* We are expected to reply to these invitations whether we are able to attend or not.

If the invitations say, "Regrets only," we need only reply if we cannot attend.

If we accept an invitation and later discover we cannot attend, we notify our hostess as soon as possible.

# Pre-dinner Social Time

Often before dinner our hostess will serve beverages and hor d'oeuvres (appetizers). This gives guests time to gather and introduce themselves to one another.

**Hints:**

* We don't set our glass down on a table without using a coaster.

* Any pits, stems, or other disposables should be put into a napkin unless another way of disposing of them is provided.

* With dips, only dip once per chip.

* We should save room for our dinner, no matter how good the appetizers are.

# Mealtimes Are Special

We can be sure our hostess has spent a lot of time and effort on our meal. In return, it's only polite to come to the table properly dressed, with clean hands and combed hair.

By practicing good table manners at home, we will learn what is expected and feel comfortable in more formal circumstances.

Food is served several different ways at dinner parties:

After everyone is seated at the table, the food is passed around the table in serving dishes. Sometimes the host or hostess will serve the meat dish.

The food is placed on a serving table. If it is a large party, guests help themselves and occasionally eat off their laps or small tables.

A waiter or waitress brings the serving dishes to each person at the table, *or*, the food is placed on the plates elsewhere and brought to you at the table.

# Table Settings

The way forks, knives, spoons, glasses, and cups are placed on the table is a "table setting."

The one shown here is a *formal* place setting. We naturally don't use all of this each day at home. However, it shows us where each piece is placed, whether we have eight pieces of silver or three.

We use the silver from the *outside in.* For example, the soup spoon on the right would be used before the teaspoon, because soup is served first.

Although table settings will vary, depending on where we are eating, we want to use good table manners at all times.

At a
buffet, plates
are usually stacked
at the beginning of
the serving table.
Sometimes the silverware
is wrapped in
napkins on the
serving table;
other times,
it will be at
your table.

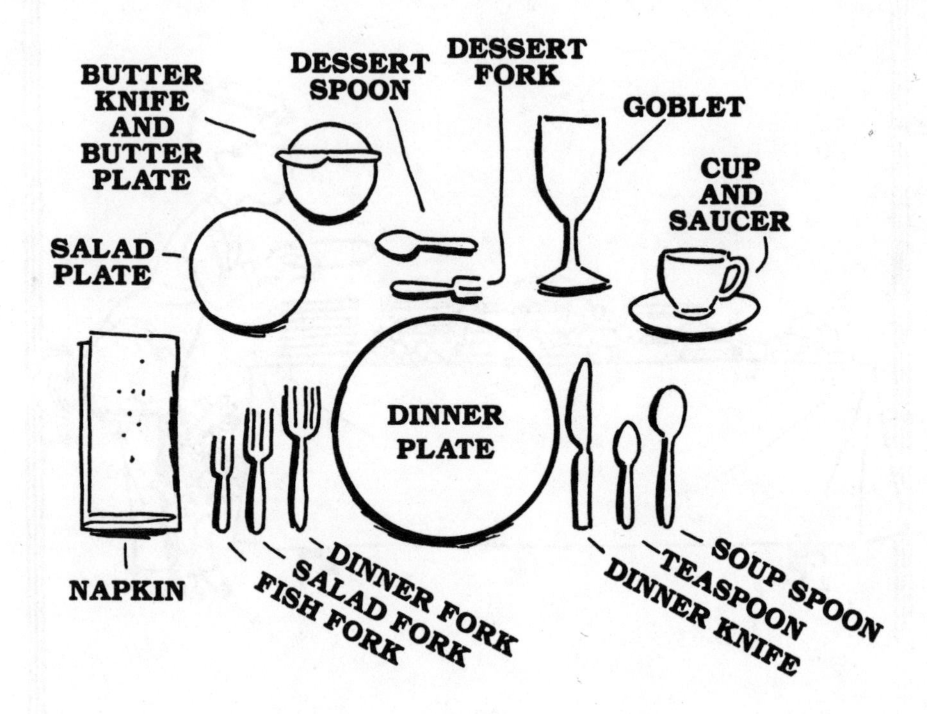


## Silverware

Silverware is used from the outside in, with the first fork on the left being used first and the first spoon on the right being used first. A spoon or fork placed above our dinner plate is used for dessert.

If the setting is confusing we should just watch our hostess and use what she uses. If we begin to use the wrong utensil, we don't worry about it — we just continue to use it for that course.

**Glasses**

Use the glass to the right of our plate. Large stemmed glasses are called *goblets*. Hold by the bowl, not the stem, to avoid spills.

A glass without a stem is held in the middle, not at the rim.

If we need to pass a glass or cup to someone, we don't touch its rim with our fingers.

**Bread and Butter Plate (1)**

This is located on our left, slightly above our plate. Use this plate for rolls, butter, olive pits, and so forth. Our butter knife will be on this plate and should be left there after you use it.

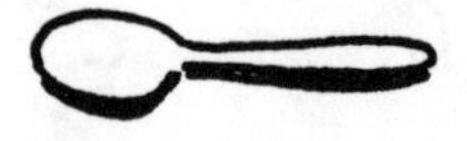

**Salad Plate (2)**

Your salad plate is also to the left of your dinner plate, slightly below the bread and butter plate.

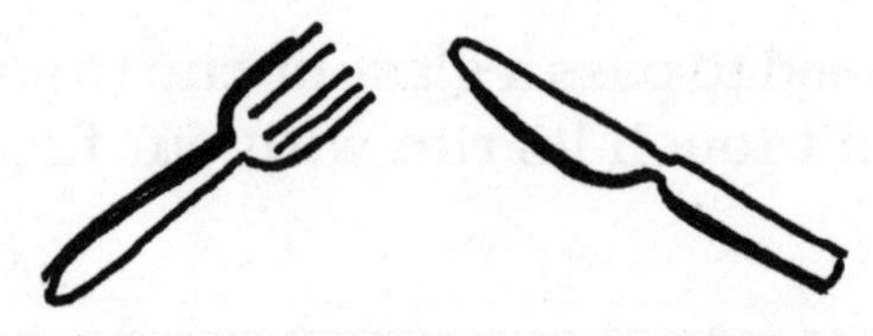

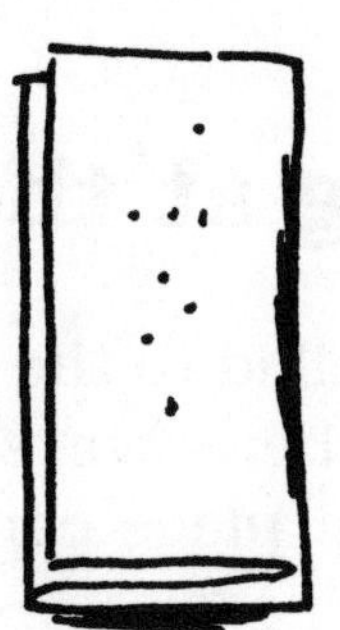

**Napkin**

Our napkin is usually to the left of our dinner plate. Occasionally it will be folded on our plate or in our glass.

The first thing we do when we sit at the table is to place our napkin *on our lap*.

- A *large* dinner napkin is opened in half with the fold on top. The open bottom half may be used to blot our mouth.

- A *small* luncheon napkin may be opened all the way.

- Remember, a napkin isn't meant to be a bib, towel, or handkerchief. We never blow our nose in a napkin. We use napkins to blot or wipe our mouth.

## Sitting at the Table

When we are called to the table, our hostess will indicate where we should sit, unless there are formal place cards by each plate.

It's considered polite to stand behind our chair at the table until our hostess is seated or asks us to sit.

Boys should help the girls next to them be seated by pulling out their chairs and easing them back toward the table — gently, please!

**Basic Table Rules**

* Sit up straight.

* No chair rocking.

* Keep our feet to ourself. No kicking or sprawling.

* Napkins go on our lap, not under our chin.

## Grace

Many people begin their meals by saying a prayer of thanks. It may be referred to as "Grace," "The Blessing," or "Returning Thanks."

We wait to see if grace will be said before we begin to eat. Some sample graces are:

> *"Our Father, we thank You for this food. Make us mindful of the needs of others. In Jesus' name. Amen."*

> *"God is great, God is good. Let us thank Him for our food. Amen."*

# Enjoying the Meal

We must remember to wait for our hostess to lift her fork before we begin to eat — or until she tells us to begin. At a large dinner party of more than 8-12, we may begin to eat after four or five people have been served.

Forks and spoons are held more like a pencil than a shovel, and it's not polite to wipe silverware clean with our napkin (if it really needs it, we wipe it discreetly, under the table).

**Bread and Butter Plate**

* Rolls, bread, butter, or jelly are all placed on the bread and butter plate.

* Break off a small piece of bread or roll and butter it.

As we eat it:

* We take butter from only one end of the stick.

* We take the roll closest to us when they are passed. Don't thumb through them.

**Soup**

* Soup is spooned away from us. When it's near the bottom of the bowl, we may tilt the bowl (away from us) to spoon up the rest.

* If soup is too hot, skim from the top of the bowl. We never blow on our soup and never slurp.

* We eat from the tip or side of our spoon. We don't insert the whole large soup spoon in our mouth.

* After finishing our soup, we leave the spoon in the bowl or on the plate underneath.

* If soup is served in a cup, we spoon the first few tastes, then if we wish, we may drink the rest and place the spoon on the plate below.

* If we are ever served a mug of soup, coffee, or chocolate, we never drink with the spoon in the mug.

# Passing Food

* As serving dishes are passed, we use the serving utensil provided. We must remember to return the spoon to the serving dish before passing it on.

* We must never touch the rim of a cup or glass when passing it.
* Only take as much food as you intend to eat.
* Never use your own fork or spoon to help yourself.
* We must be sure to allow enough in our portion for other guests.
* Unless our hostess indicates otherwise, we pass food counterclockwise (to your right).
* We should take a little of everything, whether we like it or not. We shouldn't ask, "What's this?" We can leave something on our plate; but we never make a fuss about it. If we don't like certain food, we can think "yuk," but don't say it.

**Cutting Food**

* We hold our fork in our left hand, tines down, and cut with the knife in our right hand, bearing down as we cut. If it is tough, we use a short sawing motion.

* We should cut one or two pieces at a time as we eat.

* We shouldn't make wings of our elbows as we cut.

* If the meat is tough, it's better to cut it in very small pieces.

* Salad greens may be cut if they seem too large.

* Fried chicken is finger food on a picnic, but cut with a knife and fork in a dining room unless the hostess gives permission otherwise.

## GENERAL TABLE MANNERS

* We sit up straight and bring our food to our mouth, not our mouth to our food.

* We feed ourself with one hand and leave the other on our lap.

* We must always chew with our mouth *closed.* No one wants to hear us eat or see our masticated food.

* Take small bites and drink slowly.

* We never talk with a full mouth.

* If something we have taken is too hot, we never spit it out. The best remedy is a quick sip of cold water.

* If something is stuck in a tooth, it's best ignored until after the meal, or ask to be excused and remove it elsewhere. Toothpicks are acceptable at home, but not in public.

* Gravy may be enjoyed by using a small piece of bread or roll to sop it up with.

* The tip of our knife or a small piece of bread may help us push small bits of food onto our fork.

* If we would like seconds after everyone is served, we may ask politely and pass our plate, leaving the fork and knife pointing into the center of the plate so they don't fall off.

* We should pace our eating so we finish about the same time as everyone else. We don't gobble . . . we don't dawdle.

* If we need to blow our nose, we go ahead and blow it modestly and get it over, or ask to be excused and leave the table.

* If we need to attend to something personal, we just ask to be excused without any announcements.

* Used knives and forks are never placed on the table, always kept on our plates.

* Elbows may be rested on the table during courses or at the end of the meal, but we shouldn't lean on the table at any time.

* Sometimes burps happen — hopefully quietly. If they do, we quietly say "Excuse me" and go on. We don't laugh at a burp, stomach rumble, or any other noise. Just pretend it didn't happen.

* No matter how they beg, we don't feed pets at the table.

* If we spill something, we should apologize and offer to help clean it up, but don't die of embarrassment.

* When we squeeze lemon into a drink or food, we should cup our other hand around it to guard the squirt.

* A pit, bone, or a piece of gristle may be removed with our fingertips or the tip of our fork and placed on the side of our dinner or bread and butter plate. We never spit anything out.

In wondering how something should be removed from our mouth, think . . .
Did it go in by hand? . . . . . Out by hand.
Did it go in by fork? . . . . . . . Out by fork.

* When we are finished, we place our knife and fork together in our plate, tips pointing down in the center of our plate.

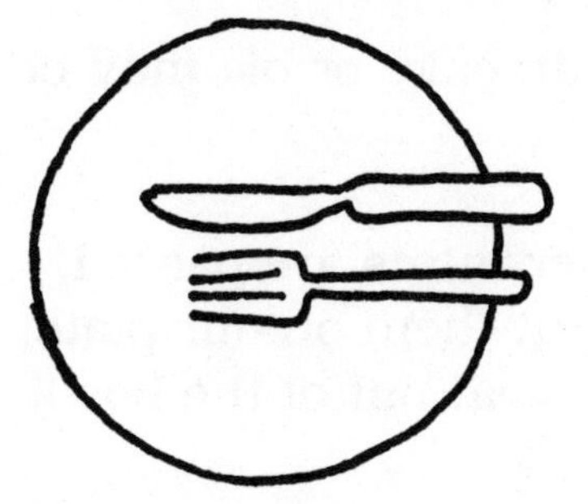

This tells a waiter that we are finished and keeps the utensils from falling on the floor when the plate is picked up.

## DESSERT

* Ice cream or other soft desserts are eaten with spoons. When we are done, we leave our spoon on the plate under the ice cream dish.

* Ice cream served with cake or pie may be eaten with a fork.

* If nuts or after-dinner mints are passed, we take a few and put them on our plate. We don't continue to eat out of the bowl!

* Fruit centerpieces are not meant to be eaten unless offered by our hostess.

**CONVERSATION**

We come to the table not only for food for our bodies. There's food for our spirits to be shared as well. Every meal gains more flavor when we add a generous portion of good conversation.

* Talk to the person seated next to you at the table as you eat — but not when your mouth is full.

* Dinner-table conversation should be light and pleasant. Don't get into arguments or tell gory stories at the table. No one is really interested in every detail about the book you just read.

* We never gesture with food in our hands or on our utensils while we are talking.

## AFTER THE MEAL

* We must always remember to thank the hostess and compliment her on the meal.
* It's nice to offer help in cleaning up.
* When we leave the table, we place our napkin at the side of our plate (don't refold it) and push our chair back under the table.
* At home, we never leave the table without being excused. It's always nice to tell Mom, who cooks every day, that we appreciate her cooking too. (A kiss is even better.)

**Before we sit down:**

* Dress nicely
* Have clean hands
* Understand how the food will be served

**Beginning the meal:**

* Place napkin in lap
* Thank God
* Wait for our hostess to eat
* Use the correct utensils

**Enjoying the meal:**

* Pass food to the right
* Chew with a closed mouth
* Never talk with a full mouth
* Ask politely for food to be passed
* Use good posture
* Enjoy good conversation

**Here's a chapter you can really sink your teeth into.**

***"When it comes to eating, you can sometimes help yourself more by helping yourself less."***

*Richard Armour*

***"Eating slowly helps to keep one slim; in other words, haste makes waist."***

*A. H. Hallock*

**"Mealtime is that period of the day when kids sit down to continue eating."**

# Chapter 4

# Restaurant Manners

Fast Food

Family Restaurant

Cafeteria

Fine Dining

Everyone enjoys eating out. We can assume that everyone else in the restaurant is there for a pleasant experience, too. We want to be considerate of those around us and those who serve us. Restaurant managers strive to create the best possible dining atmosphere. When we use our good manners, we help to maintain a pleasant atmosphere.

> ***"We don't sell food. We sell happiness."***
> *Howard Johnson*

The table manners we discussed in the preceding chapter all apply to restaurant dining, too.

- When we order, we say, "May I please . . ."
- When we're served, we say, "Thank you."
- We always control the level of our voices.
- We don't make unnecessary noises that would disturb others.

There are basically four types of restaurants.

No matter where we eat,
everyone in the restaurant has a treat
when we use our good manners.

# Fast Food Restaurants

- When ordering in any restaurant, we want to be courteous to the person taking our order, using good manners passwords such as "Please" and "Thank you."
- We should know exactly what we want to order before reaching the head of the line, especially if there are a lot of people waiting behind us.
- We take only the amount of napkins, straws, and condiments that we'll need. We never waste.
- If there is not a place mat at our table, we open a napkin and place our food on it for sanitary reasons.
- Sometimes a place mat is placed on our food tray for that purpose.
- We collect our trash and dispose of it in the bin provided as we leave.

# CAFETERIA

- Selecting our meal in a cafeteria is a fun experience. There are always more choices than we can possibly eat, and we can sometimes reach the end of the line with a tray too full for our stomachs. It's helpful if we know the selections before we have to choose. That way our selections match both our tastes and our appetites.

- When we reach our table with our food and silverware, we "set our place" exactly as we would at home.

- Most cafeterias have people to collect trays. If not, we simply place our trays on the nearby tray stand.

- Most cafeterias also provide people to clean tables. Again, if no one is available to do this, we want to take care of it ourselves in consideration of the next people to use our table.

# FAMILY RESTAURANTS

- Family restaurants offer sit-down dinners. That is, we don't stand in line for our food as we do for fast-food or in a cafeteria. The food is brought to us. Family restaurants have a much larger selection of food than fast-food restaurants and are more affordable than a gourmet restaurant.
- When we're shown to our table, we'll usually find our silverware wrapped in our napkin. In such a case, it's our job to set the silverware out as we would when eating at home.
- Family restaurants do not always provide butter plates. Therefore, we put our butter and bread on our dinner plates, never on the bare table.
- As we use cracker papers or butter wrappings, we place the empty material in the ashtray or under our plates.
- When we speak to the person who serves us, we call them "waiter" or "waitress," not "mister" or "sir." We never try to get their attention by tapping a glass, snapping our fingers, clapping hands, or above all, whistling.

# SALAD BARS

Many restaurants provide salad bars that vary in size and selection, but there are basic manners that apply to all.

- We never use our fingers to take anything from a salad bar.
- We're always as careful as possible to avoid spilling the salad selections we choose.
- If one food accidentally falls into another, carefully replace it with the tongs.
- We don't take more than we can eat or pile our plates too full. 
- We don't finger through the rolls. We select the roll we want without handling the others.
- We keep all cracker wrappers tucked neatly under our plate.

# GOURMET RESTAURANTS

A gourmet restaurant deserves the "fine dining" description. The food, decor, atmosphere, and service are all finer than other style restaurants. The prices are also higher.

None of these qualities necessarily make a gourmet restaurant a "better" restaurant, simply a different type restaurant offering a different dining experience.

It's a good idea to wear "dressier" clothes in this kind of setting. We'll definitely feel more comfortable and enjoy our visit more. It's fun to anticipate special experiences that we don't enjoy every day of the week.

- In a fine restaurant, a maitre d' will show us to our table, a bus boy will fill our water glass and serve our rolls, and a waiter or waitress will take our order and serve us. We may observe a small army of people attending our dining needs.
- If we are being "treated" to dinner, we want to be considerate of our host or hostess. We don't order the most expensive item on the menu.
- We wait to see, for example, if our host or hostess orders an appetizer, soup, salad, or dessert. All of these items cost extra and add a great deal to the total bill. If our host or hostess does not order extra items, we want to be considerate and not order them either.

- The service staff will be happy to explain menu items we don't understand.

- We want to be sure our manners are showing. We'll have many opportunities to use "Please" and "Thank you." We can expect excellent service. It's kind to show our appreciation.

- If we drop our silverware, we leave it on the floor and ask for a replacement. It's not necessary or sanitary to pick up dropped utensils.

Regardless of the type restaurant we visit, if we notice folks waiting to be seated, it's considerate not to unduly prolong our "after-dinner conversation" at our table. We can always continue our conversation elsewhere and allow the folks waiting to use our table to be seated. If the situation were reversed, we would surely appreciate this display of consideration and good manners. This is another example that manners are shown just as much by how we handle people and situations as by how we handle our knives and forks.

*Never feel embarrassed to bow your head in a restaurant and thank God for your food.*

## The Menu

There are two basic types of food service in a restaurant:

* Table d'hote: one price for a complete meal.
* À la carte: each course is priced separately.

We should read our menu carefully or inquire before ordering, if we're in doubt. A full meal includes an appetizer, soup, salad, main course (entrée), dessert, and beverage. If we know we can't eat that much, we can ask to skip one or two courses, or we may order à la carte. Many restaurants include a salad and a vegetable with our entrée. Feel free to inquire.

Many finer restaurants offer a small sorbet (sherbet) after the salad course. This chills the taste buds and clears the salad flavor for the main course, but it usually comes as a surprise to most diners (a happy one, for children).

Crackers are served with the soup course. No matter what we do at home, this is not the time to crumple up the crackers and drown them in our soup.

If our fingers become sticky, it is permissible to wet the corner of our napkin in our water glass and use it to clean our fingers. But children, ask your parents first!

# RESTAURANT NO-NOS

**We Don't**

* Use straws as blowpipes.
* Make siphons out of straws.
* Blow bubbles with straws.
* Dangle spoons from our nose.
* Play music with glasses.
* Pile dishes or assist in cleaning table.
* Build houses with packages of matches or sugar containers.
* Cut bread with small bread and butter knife.
* Write on tablecloths.
* Write *anything* in a rest room
    * Crunch ice at the table.
    * Get carried away with the ketchup bottle

**Rest Rooms**

* The fewer items we touch in a rest room, the better.
* Always flush.
* Wash our hands.
* Place towels in receptacles.
* Leave the rest room neat.

# THE CHECK/TIPPING

We want to look over our check carefully to make certain it's accurate. Some restaurants automatically include the gratuity, or tip (also known as surcharge).

We wouldn't want to overlook this detail and tip twice, regardless how good the service may have been. The standard tip is 15%. Some people tip 18% or 20% if they feel the service has been very special.

Tips are basically the major part of a waiter or waitress's salary.

If our waiter has given extremely poor service, we may want to adjust the quantity of our tip accordingly.

If we are served a meal that is clearly unacceptable, good manners do not require us to eat it. We would do ourselves and the management a favor by calling it to their attention. All well-operated restaurants will gladly replace unsatisfactory food or make a suitable adjustment.

# MISCELLANEOUS

Formal restaurants have a plate at each place or will put one there after guests are seated. This is the "service plate." Appetizers, salad or soup plates are placed on this service plate. The service plate is removed when our entrée is served.

Many folks today are diet conscious and try to avoid too many calories. We may not care to eat dessert under such circumstances. Another way is to share a dessert. Our waiter will be happy to bring one dessert and two plates. This way you can have your cake and eat it, too.

Tea is usually served in the form of a tea bag with a pot of hot water. We place the tea bag in the teapot (not our cup) and allow it to brew to the strength we want. Leave the tag on the outside of the teapot.

Remove the tea bag with your spoon, wrapping the string around it, draining water into the pot. Place the tea bag on your saucer or service plate. When the tea bag is served by the side of your cup, handle it the same way when it is removed.

# FINGER BOWL

A fine restaurant will serve a finger bowl after we have completed our meal.

We dip our fingers, one hand at a time, into the bowl and dry them on our napkin.

Occasionally a piece of lemon is in the water. We rub our fingers on this to remove any food odors that may linger from dinner.

We may touch our fingers to our lips if necessary and dry them with our napkin.

***Do We Eat It With a Fork, Spoon, or Fingers?***

Grapes, plums, cherries, celery, carrot sticks . . . . . . . . . . . . . . . . Fingers
Pickles, olives, radishes . . . . . . . . . . . Fingers
Corn on the cob . . . . . . . . . . . . . . . Fingers
French fries (fast-food, picnic) . . . . . . Fingers
French fries (dining room) . . . . . . . . . . . Fork
French fried chicken (picnic) . . . . . . Fingers
French fried chicken (dining room) . . . . Fork
Watermelon . . . . . . . . . . . . . . . . . . . . Fork
Strawberries or dessert . . . . . . . . . . . . . Fork
Cut fruit on dinner plate . . . . . . . . . . . . Fork
Dry, crisp bacon . . May be eaten with fingers
Artichoke . . . . . . . Pull each leaf with fingers to dip in butter
Lobster in shell . . . . . Parts can only be eaten by fingers

## Foreign Words on Menu

We may always ask a waiter or waitress what foreign words on menus mean. Here are some common foreign words we may run into, and what they mean.

| | |
|---|---|
| à la | in the style of |
| à la king | in cream sauce |
| almandine | with almonds |
| au jus | in its own juice |
| bernaise | sauce with tarragon |
| bisque | a type of soup, usually seafood |
| boeuf | beef |
| bon bon | candy |
| bordelaise | a brown sauce |
| bouillabaisse | fish chowder |
| braisèe | braised |
| brioche | a French yeast roll |
| cafe glacé | coffee ice cream |
| canapé | small, open-faced sandwich |
| champignons | mushroom |
| citron | lemon |
| compote de fruits | stewed mixed fruit |

## Foreign Words on Menu
*(continued)*

| | |
|---|---|
| coq au vin | chicken in wine sauce |
| crème | cream |
| crêpes | thin pancakes |
| croutons | diced toasted bread |
| demitasse | strong black coffee |
| en croute | baked in pastry crust |
| escargot | snails |
| fillet de boeuf | tenderloin of beef |
| filet mignon | grilled choice beef |
| flambée | served flaming |
| Florentine | with spinach |
| foie gras | goose liver |
| frappé | chilled |
| fromage | cheese |
| fruits de mer | seafood |
| garni | decorated |
| gateau | cake |
| gratiné | topped with bread crumbs and cheese |
| hollandaise | sauce with egg, lemon, butter |
| hor d'oeuvres | appetizers |
| julienne | thin strips |
| lait | milk |
| légumes | vegetables |
| madrilene | clear chilled soup |

## Foreign Words on Menu

*(continued)*

| | |
|---|---|
| maison | house (restaurant) |
| menthe | mint |
| Mornay | white cheese sauce |
| mousse | light dessert of cream and eggs |
| moutarde | mustard |
| oeuf | egg |
| omelette | egg dish |
| parfait | iced dessert |
| petit | small |
| poisson | fish |
| poivre | pepper |
| pomme | apple |
| potage | soup with cream base |
| poulet | chicken |
| Provençal | French stew |
| purée | mashed food |
| quiche | a tart of eggs and cheese |
| ratatouille | mixed vegetables |
| sorbet | fruit sherbet |
| soufflé | puffed dish with eggs, cheese, etc. |
| tarte | pie |
| tournedos | filet of beef |
| vichyssoise | cold potato soup |
| vinaigrette | salad dressing |

# Summary

* Always say "May I please . . .?"
* Remember your table manners.
* When served, always say, "Thank you."
* Feel free to ask politely for whatever you need.
* Be considerate of those around you.
* Always thank your host if you are a guest.
* Enjoy your special eating experience and do your best to help others enjoy theirs, too.

# Chapter 5

## Keys To Good Conversation

# Conversation

***"Speak clearly if you speak at all . . .***
***Carve every word before you let it fall."***
*Oliver Wendell Holmes*

Conversation is an exchange of *thoughts* more than *words*.

Interest in people helps us to be good conversationalists. We may not know a lot about current events or a specific topic of conversation, but we can still join in by asking polite questions and really being interested in what other people think.

The main point is to let people know we care for them. A simple way to do this is by asking people about themselves, their families, and their activities.

We want to look alert and smile as we talk to people, and when someone asks us a question in return, we should answer with more than "yes," "no," or a grunt.

It's a good idea to avoid controversial subjects. Good manners are always tactful.

* We don't ask Aunt Millie if she's as rich as the family says she is.

* We don't tell Cousin Joan she has a pimple on her nose.

* Our conversation shouldn't be centered around *ourselves, our families, our* work, *our* interests, and *our* ideas.

We want our conversation to be stimulating. We want to listen, *learn*, grow, and enjoy a lively exchange of ideas.

Good conversation is putting into practice the old saying, "Two minds are better than one."

# Good Listening

Ideally, a conversation should be give and take. Back and forth like a tennis match, each one getting a chance.

No one should monopolize a conversation.

"A person who *monopolizes* a conversation, *monotonizes* it."

As we listen, we want to focus on what is *being* said, not what *we* want to say. Good manners don't simply put on a smile while our eyes reveal our ears and minds aren't paying attention.

***"Conversation is the art of telling folks a little less than they want to know."***
*Franklin P. Jones*

When we're good *listeners*, others always consider us good *conversationalists*.

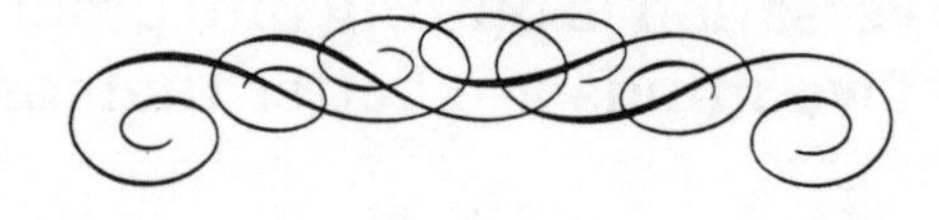

**When We Listen:**

* Look directly at the one speaking
* Be interested in what is being said
* Don't let our attention be diverted
* Don't fidget, look at our watch, yawn or show impatience
* Be responsive

**"A bore is someone who goes on talking while we're interrupting."**

We don't need to listen to talk that makes us uncomfortable.

Good manners put us at ease. We don't have to look over our shoulders when good manners are present.

We can always walk away from such things as:

* Gossip
* Dirty jokes
* Ethnic jokes
* Any conversation that talks about people in a negative way

***"Conversation between Adam and Eve must have been different. They had no one to talk about."***

# THINGS TO AVOID

Good manners lead us to say things that add to the *joy* of life. We don't want to say things that add to the *grief*.

We would never say something to deliberately hurt someone, but it's possible we might inadvertantly embarrass or offend someone. It's wise to avoid the subjects of finances, weight, size, religion or anything that might be sensitive.

If we're asked a personal question that we don't care to answer, we should feel free to say, "I'd rather not talk about that."

## Some Questions Not to Ask

- How much did that cost?
- Why do you wear your hair like that?
- How heavy is your mother?
- How much does your father make?
- Why don't you get your teeth straightened?

Braggadocio is an "I" disease. It puffs up our head and our chest. It really repells people.

***"The tongue is a small part of the body, but it makes great boasts."***
*James 3:5*

# Conversation Starters

Not everyone has the gift of gab, but there are ways around that problem. Questions are always good conversation, since they show people we are interested in them.

- ★ Where do you go to school?
- ★ How many sisters and brothers do you have?
- ★ Where do you live?
- ★ What's your favorite book?
- ★ What sports do you like?
- ★ Do you have any hobbies?
- ★ Do you like music?

Parents enjoy talking with their children, too. We have a lot more in common than we think we might, and there are many questions that we can ask to start a conversation with them.

★ Did you have a nice day, Mom?; ★ Who did you have lunch with today?; ★ What's planned for the weekend?; ★ Did you like school when you were a kid, Dad?; ★ What was your first pet, Mom?

We're living in busy, exciting days, and sometimes we have to work hard at making conversation in our homes. Families are often coming and going in different directions. Once in a while it's good to turn off the TV and other distractions and concentrate on what makes families special:

*Love, heritage, goals, memories, adventures. We all need to know our roots and how they've grown. We need to know about all the interesting folks who've been part our family tree.*

***"The most brilliant, witty person in the world may find it difficult to talk with his own relatives. Often we have the most to say to those we have the least do to with."***

*Sydney Harris*

The best place to enjoy good conversation is at the table . . . breakfast, lunch and dinner . . . with our own family. Folks often sit in silence and miss the opportunity of this special time together each day.

**Some families find that their times together at the table and their conversation seems to be much more fun and much more meaningful if they begin each meal by talking to God.**

## Compliments

Everyone enjoys a sincere compliment. It's possible someone may not be as good as we say they are, but we can be sure they'll try harder after the compliment. Compliments not only lift *people,* they lift *conversations* . . . as long as they're *sincere.*

It's not hard to find things to compliment:

- You have pretty teeth
- You're a good driver. I feel safe with you.
- Nice serve, Pat.
- It's always fun to be with you.
- Dad, that new shirt looks great on you.
- I like your dress. Do you have a favorite place to shop?
- This is a super meal, Mom.
- Your home is lovely. Did you decorate it yourself?
- How did learn to swim so well?

**A compliment really says we're not self-centered. We're interested in others and find things about them to admire.**

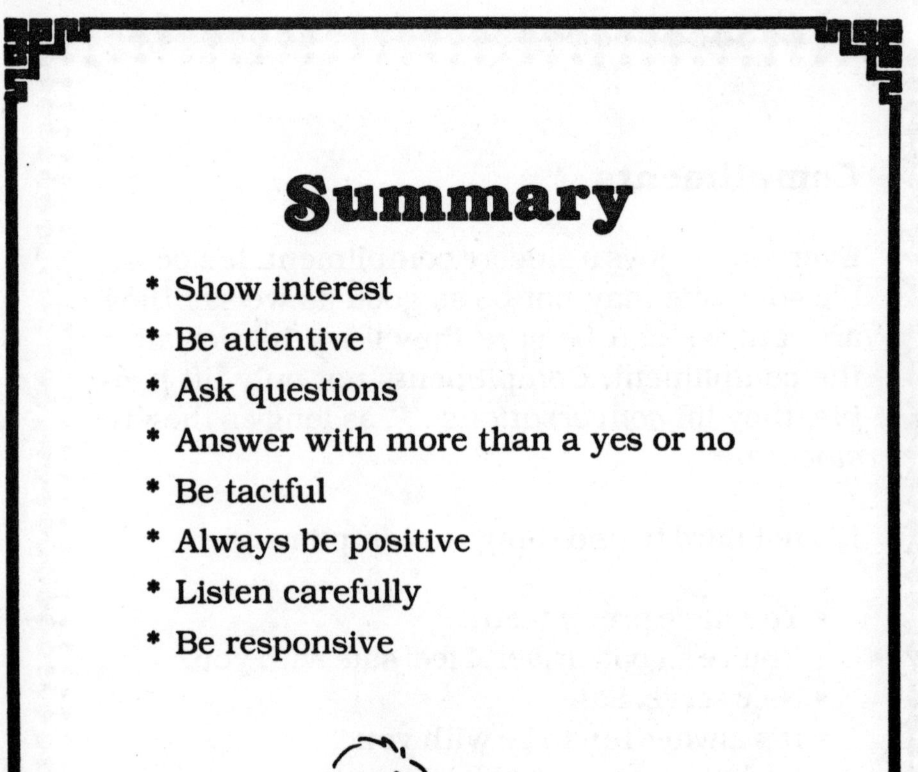

# Summary

* Show interest
* Be attentive
* Ask questions
* Answer with more than a yes or no
* Be tactful
* Always be positive
* Listen carefully
* Be responsive

Chapter 6
Telephone
Manners

# ☎ TELEPHONE MANNERS ☎

We should try to make the best impression we can on the telephone. How someone "sees" us over the telephone is important, since they may never see us in person.

Our voice reveals a lot about us — whether we're warm and friendly or cold and abrupt will come through the telephone lines. Let our voice "smile" for us.

☎

**"My teenage daughter is at the awkward age. She knows how to *make* phone calls, but not how to *end* them."**

## WHEN THE PHONE RINGS

* Say, "Hello."
* Speak clearly and distinctly.
* If the call is for someone else, say, "Just a minute, please. May I ask who's calling?" Then call the person to the phone, but don't shout!
* If the call is for someone not at home, and we're alone, it's wise not to say so. Just say, "I'm sorry, they can't come to the phone now. May I take a message or have them call back?"
* It's wise not to say we are home alone.
* When we take a message, be sure to deliver it.

  Writing the message down immediately and leaving it by the phone is a good practice.

☎ If Grandma or Grandpa call, we want to enjoy a nice chat with them before we call our parents to the phone.

Grandparents are very special, and they think we are, too! Our conversations with them mean a lot, and we want to take advantage of them while we can.

☎ We want to be friendly and exchange pleasantries with all family and friends who call, even if the call isn't for us.

That's part of good manners.

**WHEN WE MAKE A CALL**

- Always allow several rings before hanging up.
- We always identify ourself and say, "May I please speak with ______(name)______? Thank you."
- If someone we know answers the phone (not the person we're calling) we should be polite and chat with them for a minute. We never want to be too busy to be friendly.

**Example:**

*"Oh, hello, Mrs. Jones. This is John. How are you? May I please speak to Jim? Thank you. Nice to talk to you."*

(If we're calling someone of the opposite sex, this is an excellent way to impress their parents.)

# ☏ Things To Do On the Phone ☏

★ Always answer by saying HELLO.

★ Answer politely and always say good-bye.

★ We should always use words of courtesy: please, thank you, how are you?, etc.

★ Apologize when you get a wrong number.

★ Use people's names.

# ☏ Things NOT To Do ☏

★ Eat while talking.

★ Talk to others in the room with us while on the phone with another person.

★ Rattle dishes or papers while talking.

★ Answer by saying, "Yeah?", "Hold on," "Whadaya want?" or "Whoozit?"

★ Tie up the line too long.

★ Secretly listen in on someone else's call.

# Answering Machines

Answering machines are commonly used today. Whether we like them or not, they're a fact of life we must deal with.

When an answering machine receives our call, our response may be short and sweet:

- Wait for beep.
- Give our name.
- Give the time you are calling.
- Give reason for our call.
- State if your call should be returned.
- Say, "Thank you" and "Good-bye."
- Hang up.

## Call Waiting

Another new device that is available today is *Call Waiting.* When we are talking on the phone, a special tone tells us that another party is calling. By depressing the switch-hook we can put someone on "HOLD," while we answer the second call.

Unless we are expecting an important call or use our phone for business, as well, it is an imposition to use this service.

If we are called to the phone from a distance and are then put on "hold," for the convenience of the caller, we would probably consider the practice to be rather inconsiderate.

Good manners should be communicated over the phone as well as face-to-face.

All new technology is designed to make our lives better. We don't want to abuse our relationships by misusing gadgets designed for convenience.

Good manners will always be the art of using everything available to us in a way that improves our lives and relationships.

# Summary

We want to:

- Have a smile in our voice.
- Use people's names on the phone.
- Use courteous words.
- Speak clearly.
- Always say good-bye.
- Remember, the telephone is not a toy.

# Chapter 7

# Family Manners

Where there is life, there should be love. Especially family love. Love makes a house a home. Size, color, location have nothing to do with the spirit that dwells inside.

A family and its manners are shaped by the quality of the spirit they share. A spirit based on love makes a happy home and always produces good manners.

When a child feels love, understanding and genuine recognition, many of the problems of delinquency are avoided.

***"When parents have little time for children, a great vacuum will develop and some kind of ideology will move in."***

*Billy Graham*

Manners aren't taught in school. Children learn manners at home. They study their parents.

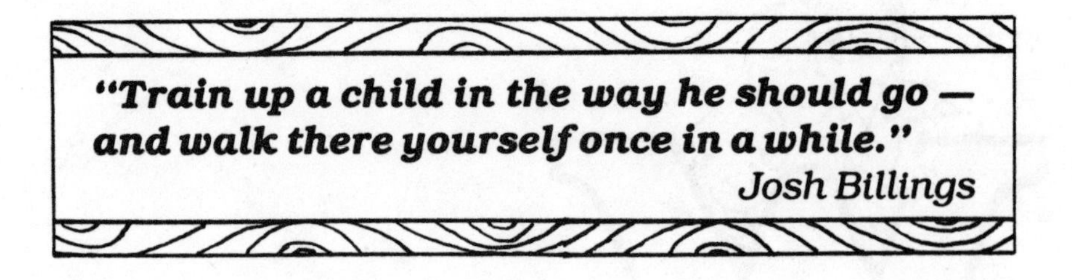


The learning process begins in the cradle. It's quickly evident that a child doesn't have to be *taught* to be bad. They have to be taught to be *good.* If a parent doesn't teach, a child will tend to go as far as it can . . . in the wrong direction.

We all make footsteps everyday. We want to make sure our footsteps are the kind we want our loved ones to follow.

Love
Honest
Considerate
Pure

Hate
Deceitful
Selfish
Polluted

Children learn best by example.

They mimic what they see.

The parent who loves always teaches and trains.

No discipline is a sign of no love.

> *"Fathers, don't provoke your children; instead, bring them up in the training of the Lord."*
>
> see Ephesians 6:4

> ***"Children have more need of models than of critics."***
>
> *Joseph Joubert*

## Many Lessons in Life Are Caught Not Taught

If a child lives with criticism,
He learns to condemn.

If a child lives with hostility,
He learns to fight.

If a child lives with ridicule,
He learns to be shy.

If a child lives with shame,
He learns to feel guilty.

If a child lives with tolerance,
He learns to be patient.

If a child lives with encouragement,
He learns confidence.

If a child lives with praise,
He learns to appreciate.

If a child lives with fairness,
He learns justice.

If a child lives with security,
He learns to have faith.

If a child lives with approval,
He learns to like himself.

If a child lives with acceptance and friendship, he learns to find love in the world.

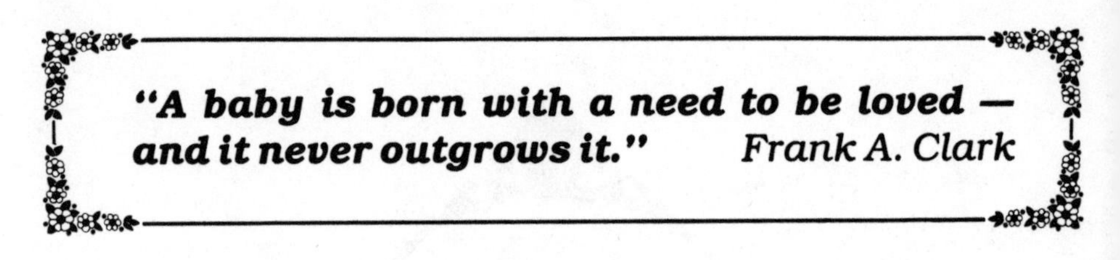

***"A baby is born with a need to be loved — and it never outgrows it."*** *Frank A. Clark*

Second in importance to *love* in a family is *communication.* Families need to talk to each other, and they need to talk honestly.

It's not always easy to be completely honest. Some things might seem embarrassing to us and we'd rather not discuss them. It might seem easier, at times, to tell a "white lie" and avoid the truth. Honesty is always the best policy and the best manners, especially at home. Our manners and our character are shaped at home.

Actually, there's no such thing as "a little white lie." Little white lies grow into big black habits.

We can be sure that if someone lies *to* us, they will lie *about* us.

Lying is really a disease that is best healed in the beginning. Good manners are healthy.

Good manners make good listeners. Our family can't enjoy communication if no one is listening.

It often seems easier to "*speak up*" than to *listen* in our families, and our manners can become sloppy.

We let our hair down at home. We relax. We live in close quarters and sometimes rub each other the wrong way.

We're vulnerable to hurt and upset. Then a pity party begins.

We forget that love is a very unselfish quality of life. We forget all about good manners and think selfishly.

We look for blame rather than balm. The closeness in a home that causes friction shouldn't overshadow the closeness that makes a family.

Family love, support and forgiveness are far greater than our hurts.

**No one knows you like a brother,**
**No one loves you like a mother,**
**No one trusts you like a sister,**
**No one cares for you like a father.**

***"Train a child in the way he should go . . .***

***. . . and when he is old he will not turn from it."***

*Proverbs 22:6*

***"There are two disappointments in life:***

**1. Not getting everything we want.**
**2. Getting everything we want."**

*Mark Twain*

The wisest man
who ever lived said:

*My son, keep your father's commands and do not forsake your mother's teaching."* Proverbs 6:20

It naturally hurts to be corrected or denied something we want very badly, but the biggest handicap parents can impose on a child is to make life too easy.

A parent may need to withhold many things, but never love. A child may need to accept limits on his desires, but always in love.

***"Don't be discouraged if your children reject your advice. Years later they will offer it to their own offspring."***

# Honor Your Parents

Fathers and mothers deserve respect. They don't need to *qualify* for it — they earned it when they gave us life. How do we honor our parents? We ...

- Ask for their advice
- Look at things from their perspective
- Try to please them
- Have a good attitude
- Show respect
- Thank them
- Compliment them
- Obey them

Parents need our honor. They want to know they have our support, just as we want to know we have their's.

> ***"Children, obey your parents in the Lord: for this is right. Honor thy father and mother."***
>
> *Ephesians 6:1, 2*

## Sisters and Brothers

We often spend more time with our sisters and brothers than we do with anyone else. We also may have more problems with them than we have with others! Many of these problems can be avoided if we:

- 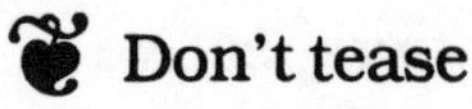 Don't tease
-  Don't be sarcastic
- 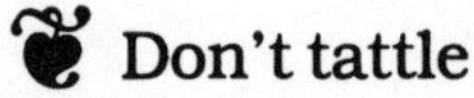 Don't tattle
- Showed love
- Helped one another
-  Picked up for one another
-  Didn't worry about "favorites"
-  Didn't count chores
- Didn't say things like, "Why make me? He didn't have to!"
-  Don't mock
-  Stick up for one another

# "Love Has Manners"

***"Love cures people — both the ones who give it and the ones who receive it."***
*Karl Menninger*

Manners show in:

- The way we speak to those we love
- The tone of our voice
- The things we say and later regret
- Our compassion for each other
- Our support for those we love
- The ways we help each other

When we feel good about ourselves, we can reach out and help others. Helping others should always start with our own family.

# Showing Our Love for Family

## For Grandparents

Respect them, write to them. Always remember to thank them, and tell them you love them.

***"Did you ever notice that grandchildren don't carry pictures of their grandparents?"***

*Charlie Jarvis*

## For Parents

Take out the garbage, do the dishes, volunteer to do chores. Better yet, do chores without complaining! Have a grateful attitude, a cheerful, cooperative spirit — this will help parents the most.

## For Brothers and Sisters

Show interest, love, and concern for them. Compliment and uphold them. Root for them. Offer to help them with their chores.

It often seems
easier to *fight*
each other than
to *love*
each other.

That's where
manners come in.
They help us
to behave and
react in ways
that are best
for everyone.

Manners make
things better.
They help us
*Enjoy* life.

Love has manners

# Summary

## Family Manners

★ Home is where the heart is.

★ Family love should be a close love.

★ Manners are caught more than taught.

★ Support one another.

★ Parents are models for their children.

★ Love will find a way.
Indifference will find an excuse.

## Chapter 8

# *People Manners*

We use good manners out of respect for ourselves and others, not because *others* are courteous, but because *we* are.

Even those who are rude to us should be treated politely. We shouldn't let a rude person create the atmosphere around us. Good manners should always be positive and always prevail.

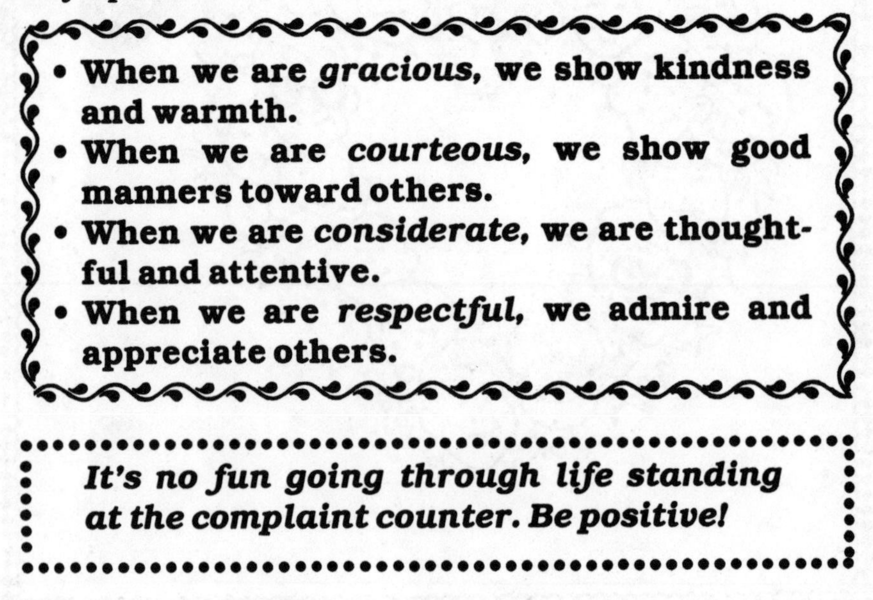

- **When we are *gracious*, we show kindness and warmth.**
- **When we are *courteous*, we show good manners toward others.**
- **When we are *considerate*, we are thoughtful and attentive.**
- **When we are *respectful*, we admire and appreciate others.**

***It's no fun going through life standing at the complaint counter. Be positive!***

# Graciousness

**We show that we're gracious when we:**

- Ask, "May I please?"
- Respond, "Thank you."
- Say, "Excuse me?" or "Sir?" or "Ma'am?" When we don't hear what was said.
- Say, "Excuse me" when we walk in front of someone.
- Say, "I'm sorry. Excuse me, please?" When we bump into someone.
- Never interrupt.
  If we have something really important to say, or if it's an emergency, we naturally may interrupt by saying, "Excuse me, but . . ." (and then we mention the urgent message).

- Respond to a compliment by saying, "Thank you."
- Cover our mouth if we sneeze, cough or yawn and then excuse ourself.
- Offer our chair to an older person who doesn't have one.
- Never use foul language.
- Never discuss body functions crudely.

# Courteousness

**We show we're courteous when we:**

- Apologize and ask forgiveness if we hurt someone or make a mistake (the quicker the easier).
- Never tell little white lies or exaggerate.
- Look for the good in people and find it.
- Lift the spirit of others.
- Treat handicapped people with the same respect we give others.
- Open and hold doors for others.
- Assist others with their coats or packages.

There are many girls who like to be treated as "ladies." They appreciate the courtesy shown by "gentlemen."

**"Ladies" appreciate "gentlemen" who:**

- Open doors for them.
- Assist them with their coats.
- Help carry their books and packages.
- Walk on the outside of the sidewalk nearest the curb.
- Carry their open umbrella.
- Stand aside and permit women to leave an elevator first.

# Consideration

**We show consideration when we:**

- Don't annoy others with a loud voice or radio.
- Respect the opinions of others.
- Don't crack knuckles, pop gum or crunch ice in front of others.
- Return what we borrow (in good condition).
- Befriend unpopular people.
- Are prompt for our appointments.
- Never draw attention to those who are different in any way.
- Pick up things that don't belong on the floor.
- Don't slam doors.
- Go up and down stairs quietly.

> ***"Carefully avoid in yourself those things which annoy you in others."***
>
> *Thomas à Kempis*

## Respectfulness

**We show we're respectful when we:**

- Never contradict our parents in public. (When parents say, "No," we want to accept it as a *positive* no. We don't want to pester.)

- Show proper respect for our elders and all in authority.

- Give others the same respect we appreciate from them.

- Make everyone in our presence comfortable.

- Apply the Golden Rule.

# Sports Courtesy

**We show we're good sports when we:**

- Never cheat.
- Don't get mad if we lose.
- Don't blame a loss on our teammates.
- Always congratulate the winner.

***"When the One Great Scorer comes, To write against our name, He asks not if we won or lost,***

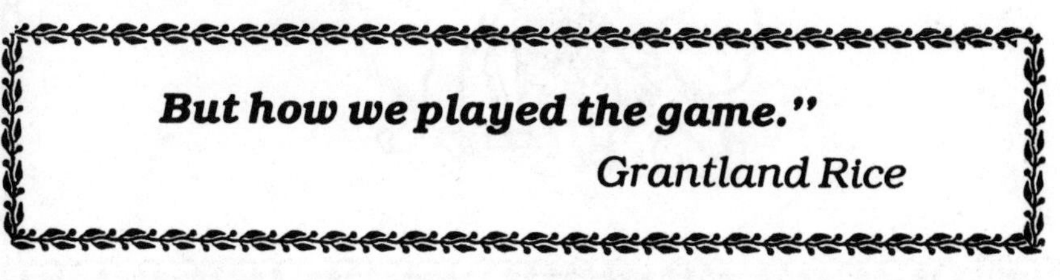

***But how we played the game."***

*Grantland Rice*

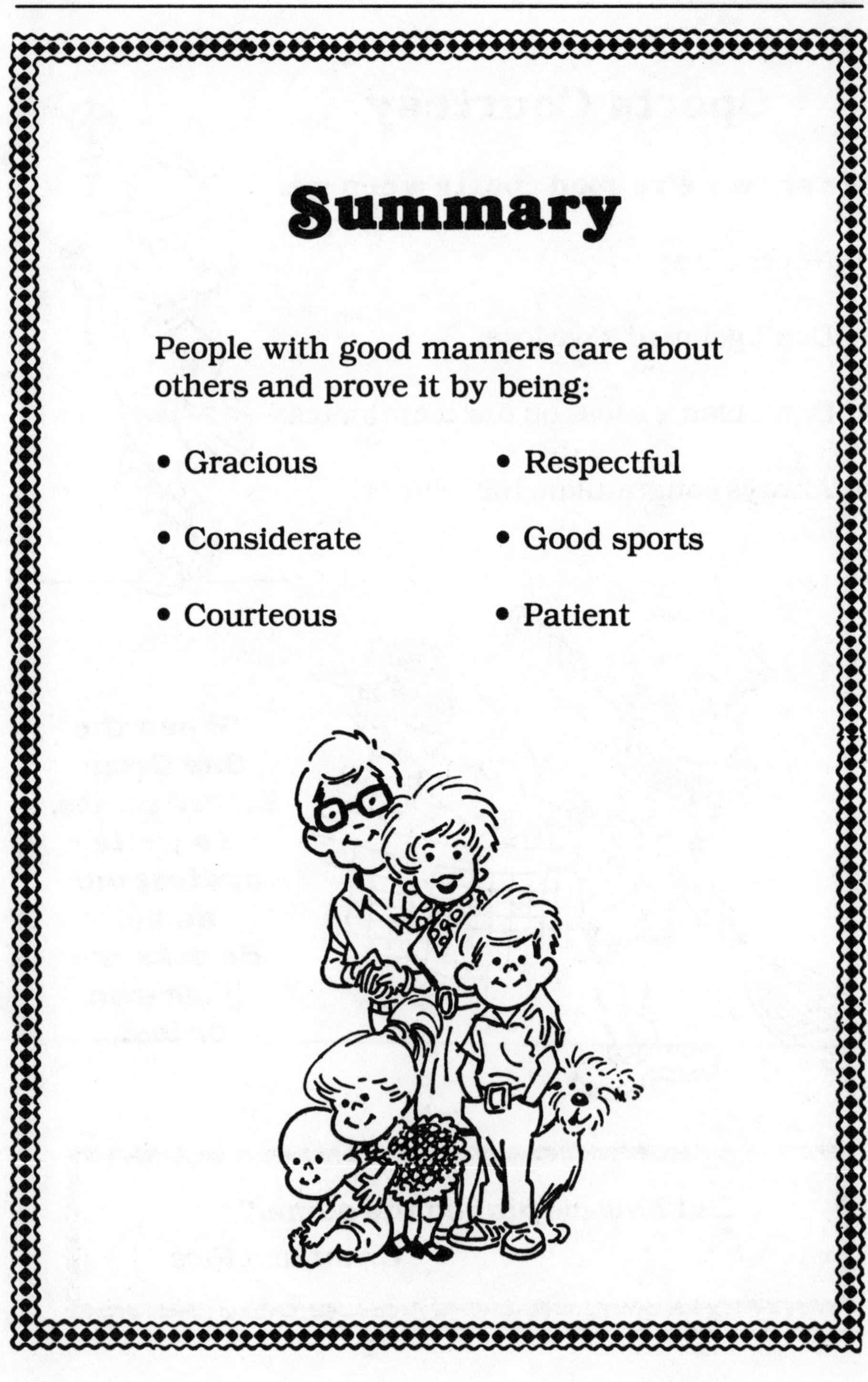

# Summary

People with good manners care about others and prove it by being:

- Gracious
- Considerate
- Courteous
- Respectful
- Good sports
- Patient

Chapter 9
Baby-Sitting

As baby-sitters, we're in charge of much more than diapers, bottles and toys . . . we're in charge of a life.

Baby-sitting is one of the most important jobs in the world.

When we're asked to baby-sit, we're being paid far more than a fee! We're being paid a tremendous compliment.

Parents are trusting us with their most valuable possessions . . . their children and their home.

---

***"A baby-sitter who's on her toes doesn't do much sitting."***

*Franklin P. Jones*

---

Whether parents say it or not, they're actually telling every baby-sitter:

**I believe the following about you:**

- You're honest
- Trustworthy
- Capable
- Responsible
- Intelligent
- Loving
- Qualified
- Compassionate

It gives us a lot to think about, doesn't it?

***"What's done to children, they will do to society."***

*Kark Menninger*

**There are certain things we need to know before the parents leave.**

**Older Children:**

♥ Are the children permitted to play outside?

♥ Are they allowed to go swimming?

♥ Should they bathe before bedtime?

♥ Are they to be fed?

♥ Can they watch TV?
a. For how long?
b. Program restrictions?

♥ Is there homework?

♥ Can they have snacks?

**Children are like mosquitoes —the minute they stop making noises you know they're getting into something.**

**Babies**

- Does the baby need a bottle?
- Should bottle be warmed?
- Does the baby need more than a bottle?
  What?
  When?
  How much?
- Where are the diapers?
- May we take baby for a walk?

***"There was never a child so lovely, but his mother was glad to get him asleep."***

*Ralph Waldo Emerson*

## Before the Parents Leave

- Where can they be reached?
- Neighbor's phone number?
- What are the phone numbers for fire and police?
- Do we need a doctor's phone number?
- Street address of home in case 911 is called?

***"When I approach a child, he inspires in me two sentiments: tenderness for what he is, and respect for what he may become."***

*Louis Pasteur*

# House Care

Our first responsibility is to the children, but we're also responsible for the house. We're expected to care for *both.*

**DO**

* Clean up after the children

* Keep toys picked up

* Leave the kitchen neat, and clean any dishes we use.

* Leave the home looking as well or better than when we arrived.

**DON'T**

* Use the phone without permission

* Tie up the telephone at any time

* Have friends in without permission

* Help yourself to food and drinks without permission.

# Telephone Messages

* Make notes of who has called
* Mark down the time of the call
* Take the telephone number of the caller
* Note when the call should be returned
* Take down any message
* It is usually not wise to say we are the baby-sitter. Just say the parents can't come to the phone right now and will call them back later.

**We want to:**

* Be kind to the children

* Give them first priority

* Follow all instructions

* Write down phone messages

* Keep everything neat

* Remember we have custody of a treasure

Chapter 10
GUEST
MANNERS

When we are invited to some-else's home as a guest, there are a few things we should remember. We need to treat the home with respect and remember that it is their home, not ours. We . . .

* Wipe our feet before entering or leave dirty shoes at the door.
* Hang up our coat properly.
* Don't slam doors or run up and down stairs.
* Don't look in anyone's closets or dresser drawers.
* Don't try on anyone's clothes or use their perfume.
* Don't turn on the TV, radio, or VCR unless invited to.
* Don't touch ornaments in the home — just look.
* Don't put our feet on furniture.
* Clean up and put things we use away.

* Never ask for food. If it's offered, remember our manners.

* If we are offered snacks, we always put any wrappers in the trash.

* If the snacks are messy, we should eat them at the table.

* If hands get sticky, we should ask where to wash them before touching anything.

* When washing our hands we don't want the dirt to end up on the guest towel; get them clean.

## AS A HOST OR HOSTESS

* It's impolite to snack on something unless we offer some to our guest.

* If we have friends in and there aren't enough snacks to go around, we should save it until they leave.

## Overnight Guests

As an overnight guest, we should always bring along our best behavior and respect the privacy and possessions of our hosts.

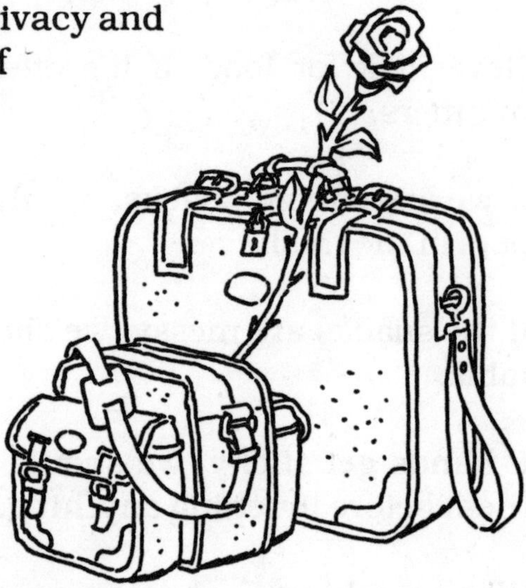

* It's good to know ahead, how long we're to stay.
* We knock before entering a closed door.
* We don't leave our things all over the house.
* Respect the house curfew.
* Watch the noise level.
* Keep the bathroom neat.
* Fold towels neatly and put them on the bars.
* Help clean up and make our bed.
* Thank our friend and his parents when we leave.
* Leave nothing behind but good impressions.
* We shouldn't overstay our welcome.
* Obviously, all of the manners listed on the previous page also apply for overnight guests.

# Swim Parties

* Bring our own towel and plastic bag for our wet suit.
* We obey all pool rules.
* We don't leave wet towels or suits on any furniture.
* We help to keep the pool area clean.
* Collect all our belongings before we leave.
* Thank our hostess.

# Summary

* As a guest, we respect others' property.
* Always bring along our best manners, for an afternoon, day or week.
* We share what we have.
* Obey house rules.
* As an overnight guest, we should check for all our belongings before leaving.
* Obey pool rules when swimming and watch wet suits on furniture.

Chapter 11
Thank You Notes

When we give someone a gift, we try to give them something we feel they will really like. We use money that we've earned and saved to buy the gift.

We wrap it nicely and present it to them with a smile and great expectations.

We just can't wait to see their reaction and, hopefully, to see a smile light up their face. Their "Thank you" is music to our ears.

The people who send us gifts feel the same way, especially if they live far away and have mailed the gift to us. They want to know that it arrived safely and that we love it. We could call them on the telephone to say thanks, and that would be better than nothing, but there's something even more special we can do — send a thank-you note.

For any gesture of kindness shown to us — a visit, a gift, or anything that made us feel good — we should try to send a thank-you note as soon as possible. If we don't show people how much we appreciate their kindness, they may think we don't care and stop doing nice things for us.

Of course we don't send thank-you notes in order to receive more presents. We write thoughtful notes because we have good manners.

Thank
You
Notes
are for:
* Dinner parties or luncheons
* Overnight visits
* Special gifts
* Special treats
* Special favors
* All gifts received by mail
* Or whenever you feel grateful
to someone for a special kindness

In the thank-you note, be sure to mention the gift you received or the kindness thc person showed to you.

## Samples

Dear Mary,

Thank you for inviting me to your birthday party. It was fun. Tell your mom I loved the cake.

Love,
Muffy

Dear Jean,

Thanks for remembering my birthday. I love the perfume you sent me. Hope you have fun at camp.

Your friend,
Mary

Dear Grandma,

Thanks so much for the mittens you made for me. I love the color, and they fit fine. Send my love to Gramps.

Love,
Jean

Dear Mrs. Jones,

Thanks so much for taking me to the shore with you. It was a lot of fun. My mom said I got a nice tan.

Sincerely,
Jimmy

*Dear Grams and Gramps,*

*I received your check in my birthday card. Thank you very much.*

*I like to get money — it always fits and is always the right color.*

*I love you and hope to see you soon.*

*Jimmy*

*Dear Mom and Dad,*

*I'm putting this note on your pillow with lots of love. I hope it helps you sleep good.*

*I sleep real good knowing you love me.*

*Your daughter,*
*Annie XXOO*

Dear Mary,

Your luncheon was beautiful; from the food to the friends.

It was nice to meet your sister; she's lovely.

Thanks so much for including me.

Fondly,
Joan

Dear Mary and John,

Bill and I had a really great time with you this weekend.

Your lake house is terrific.

Thanks so much for a wonderful visit.

With love,
Sue

# Summary

**Thank-you notes show:**

* That we received a gift sent to us.

* That we liked the gift.

* That the gift was useful for us (or fit, etc.).

* That we appreciate the gift.

* That we don't take gifts for granted.

* That we have good manners!

Chapter 12
Church
Manners

Church is a place of worship and many other wholesome, positive activities.

It's far more than a building, it's a "body-building facility with unlimited power. It builds, strengthens and encourages the body of believers."

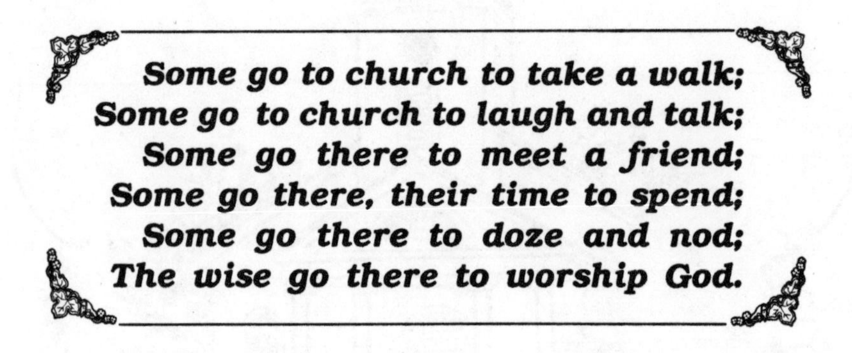

***Some go to church to take a walk;***
***Some go to church to laugh and talk;***
***Some go there to meet a friend;***
***Some go there, their time to spend;***
***Some go there to doze and nod;***
***The wise go there to worship God.***

There are several ways to make our visits to church more meaningful.

- Attend with a worshipful attitude.
- Remember God ordained the church.
- Thank God for the freedom to worship.
- Remember the church belongs to God, not man.
- Look for the ways the sermon can be relevant in your life.
- Apply the sermon to your own life, not your neighbors.
- Be involved in Sunday school and other rewarding activities.
- Ask the Lord what you can do in your church.

---

**"If a car manufacturer stops making cars, the firm goes out of business. If the Church ceases to make strong believers, it also disappears."**

---

# Our Behavior in the Sanctuary

★ Sit quietly in reverence.
★ Be on our best behavior.
★ Don't rattle papers during the service.
★ Keep our feet off pews.
★ Don't play with guest cards, envelopes, etc.
★ Keep crayons, pens off pew cushions.
★ Refrain from giggling and talking.
★ Bow our heads in prayer.
★ Sing the hymns and digest the words.
★ Above all else, worship God.

***"Going to church doesn't make us a Christian any more than going to a garage makes us a car."***

**We want to be related to God, not a building.**

# Church Socials & Suppers

This is a good time to remember our manners!

Parents should be responsible for the whereabouts of their children. Children should stay with their parents at suppers unless they have permission to leave the hall or the church building.

Sometimes children want to run to the dinner table so they may be free to play with their friends as quickly as possible. Church socials are fun times, but it's necessary for everyone to maintain some order, too.

**Things go easier when:**

- Children aren't running or pushing to be first in line.
- Children stay with parents unless they have permission to be elsewhere.
- Don't hog all your favorite food.
- Don't eat until grace has been said.
- Clean up after yourself.
- Be sure to take home any dishes you may have brought.
- We show appreciation to those who helped in the kitchen.

# A CHURCH GARDEN

Three Rows of Squash
1. Squash indifference
2. Squash criticism
3. Squash gossip

Four Rows of Turnips
1. Turn up for meetings
2. Turn up with a smile
3. Turn up with a visitor
4. Turn up with a Bible

Four Rows of Lettuce
1. Let us love one another
2. Let us welcome strangers
3. Let us be faithful to duty
4. Let us truly worship God
5. Let us give liberally

**It's interesting how a dollar can look so BIG when it goes to church, and so SMALL when it goes to the supermarket.**

Optimism is related to faith. It should abound in our places of worship. Pessimism is related to doubt. It runs rampant outside of faith. Therefore, every body of believers wants to share and multiply a faith with its eyes on God.

God wants us to "look up" and help others to do the same.

Whoever brings sunshine into the life of another, really brings sunshine into their own. The more we take the needs of others into our own heart, the more we'll take our own heart to God.

Attending church reminds us that we're not alone. We're part of the family of God. When we're hurting, the entire family hurts. When we're experiencing blessings, our church family shares them and is thankful for us.

God is a loving Father who wants the very best for His children.

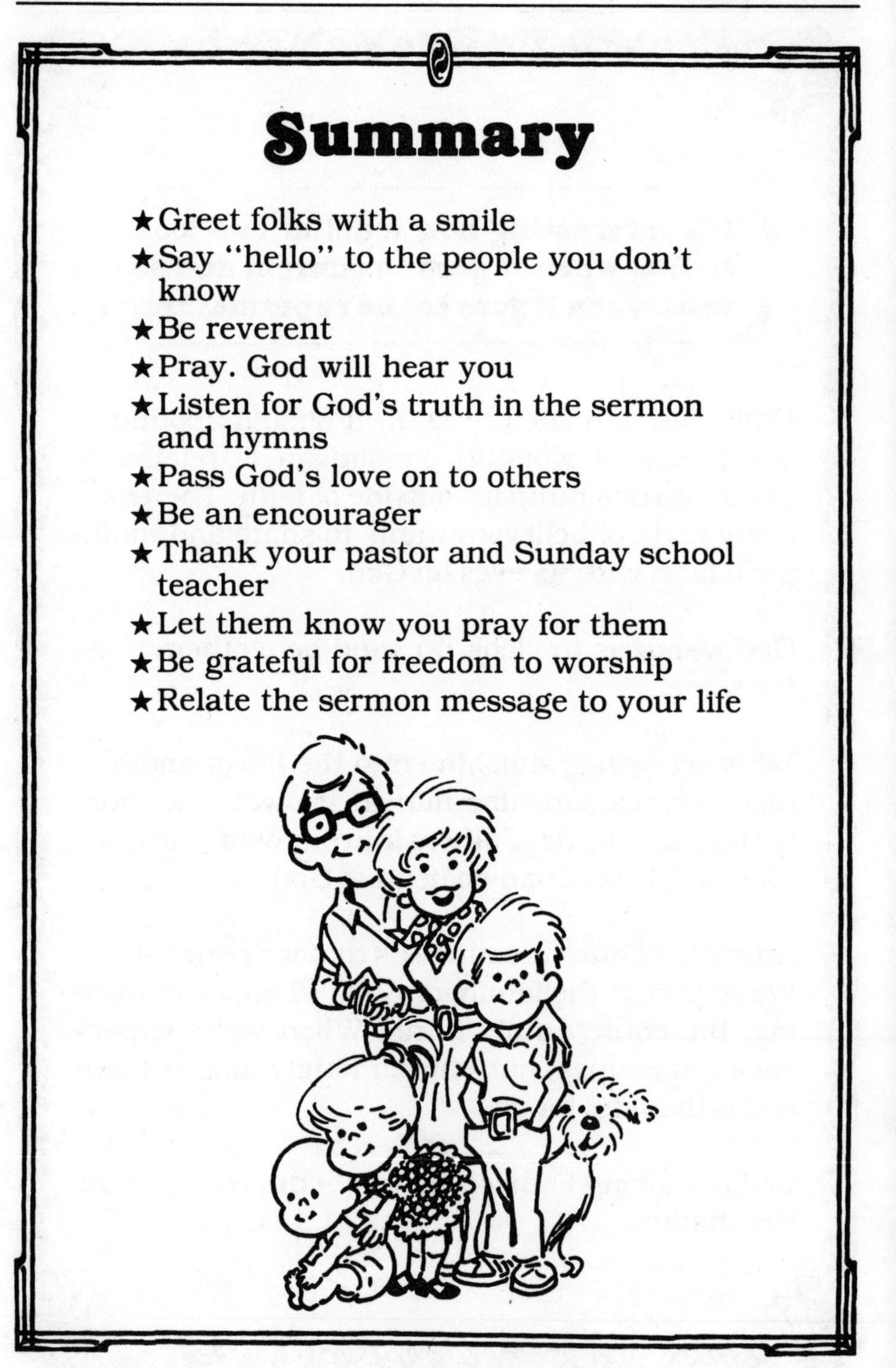

# Summary

- ★Greet folks with a smile
- ★Say "hello" to the people you don't know
- ★Be reverent
- ★Pray. God will hear you
- ★Listen for God's truth in the sermon and hymns
- ★Pass God's love on to others
- ★Be an encourager
- ★Thank your pastor and Sunday school teacher
- ★Let them know you pray for them
- ★Be grateful for freedom to worship
- ★Relate the sermon message to your life

Chapter 13
CAR TRIPS

# CAR TRIPS

Our time spent in cars sometimes seems to be as much as we spend in bed. In fact, some folks have one bed and two cars.

There's another connection between beds and cars. It's often difficult to get little children into either one of them.

Of all the rules of the road, the Golden Rule of manners is probably the most important for safe, happy motoring.

If we're "giving a lift" to someone, we treat them as our "guest" by making them feel welcome and comfortable.

If we're riding in someone else's car, we show our appreciation for their kindness and "hospitality." We display all our good manners.

It may be difficult for the driver to concentrate on the road if someone is screaming in the backseat. We want to do our part to make things pleasant for everyone.

We know that every passenger in a car is going down the same road in the same direction. Their minds, however, may be going in several different directions.

*For example:*

* **Temperature**
  What's comfortable for one may be too hot or too cold for someone else.

* **Radio**
  How loud should it be? What station shall we listen to?

* **Seating Arrangement**
  Does big brother have a better seat than we have? Who sits in the middle?

It takes good manners on the part of everyone in the car to resolve all the possible decisions that need to be made in today's high-tech cars.

Good manners in a car are easy to use. As easy as fastening a seat belt and just as safe. They work on short trips, long trips, whether we're a "guest" or a "host."

We start by recognizing that today's cars are well-equipped. They don't need backseat drivers.

The one at the wheel is in charge. They probably have their own "car rules," and we want to respect them.

If they ask us to sit in the back, we gladly sit in the back. If they prefer that we don't drink soda in the car, we don't drink soda, no matter how thirsty we seem.

## When we enter the car:

- We greet everyone with a big smile.
- We say hello, using their names.
- We fasten our seat belts.
- We remain cheerful and cooperative.
- We remember to show our appreciation.
- We look for ways to make the ride more pleasant.
    - Good conversation
    - Observe scenery
    - Fun word games

Whenever we're invited to take a long trip with friends, be sure we know how much or how little we may bring along.

**Always get the following information:**

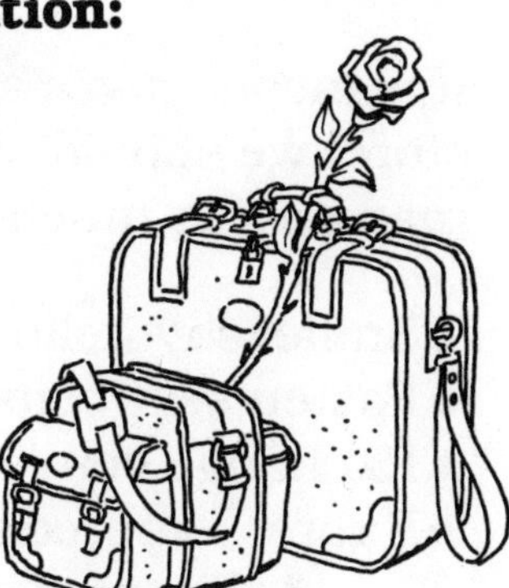

* How much luggage should I bring?
* What kind of clothing will I need?
* Should I bring my own towels and personal items?
* May I bring snacks to share?
* How much money will I need?
* When will we return?

**These things are always welcome on a car trip:**

* Seat belts fastened.
* Magic words: "Please," "thank-you," "pardon me."
* Smile (it's the best face-lift you can get).
* Simple word games that help pass the time.
* Friendliness.
* Remember to go to the bathroom before we leave.

## When We Return

* We thank the driver of the car and the person who invited us.
* Make sure we have all our belongings.
* Leave behind only a good impression.
* Say a pleasant "good-bye" to everyone in the car.
* It's thoughtful to send a "thank-you" note to the one who invited us.

## "A Short Ride"

If someone gives a "lift" from school or to the store, we should show our appreciation and manners as much as on a long ride.

★Smile, say hello
★Fasten seat belts
★Exchange conversation
★Express appreciation
★ Thank you ______NAME______

lways look up!

Everyone who drives has their eyes open for road signs. We want them to see the signs of good manners in us.

A good attitude and cooperative spirit is a sure sign of good manners.

Be creative.

Look for all the ways you can **add** to the pleasure of being together with family or friends.

A car trip is very much like every other part of life's highway. It usually turns out the way we make it.

# Never Ride With Strangers!

Good manners help us to become good passengers with folks we know.

Good sense tells us to avoid riding with anyone we **don't** know.

It's important to realize that there are dangers on the road. Not many people want to ride with **bad drivers.** No one wants to ride with **bad people!**

**Most folks *wouldn't* accept a ride from this man.**

The fact is, you can't judge a book by its cover!

Some people may seem to be friendly. They might pretend to be a friend of our parents. They might offer us money or a gift. They might say that our parents told them to "pick us up."

These might all be lies!

It's better to be **safe** than **sorry.**

**Do not,** under any circumstances, accept a ride from a stranger, no matter how nice they seem.

# Summary

Car trips are exactly what we make them.

They're either fun, pleasant experiences or they're uncomfortable, "Torture rides."

When every driver keeps his mind on the road, accidents are avoided. When we keep our minds on good manners, we avoid a car full of problems.

Poor attitudes
put pot-holes
in the road.

Smiles
smooth
the miles.

Chapter 14
Birthday
Parties

Birthday parties are fun!

They mean presents, cards, games, friends, cake and ice cream and all sorts of neat decorations.

They also mean we're a year older and at a perfect time to display our manners.

**"Some men take a day off on their birthday. Some women take a year off."**

# When We Are The Host

Spend as much time as possible with each guest at our party. We don't want to show any favoritism when we're the host.

Greet each person and be sure to introduce them to anyone they don't know.

* Thank each one with lots of enthusiasm for their gift.
* If we don't like a gift we receive, we don't reveal it.
* If we already have the very same thing, we don't reveal that, either. Good manners help us to say, "thank you," always.
* We always go to the door with each guest as they leave. We want to thank them again for helping us to celebrate and for giving us such a nice gift. (Try to name the gift.)

# When We Are A Guest

* If the birthday child answers the door, always wish them a "Happy Birthday. . ." and be sure to add their name as we present our birthday gift.
* If we're met at the door by someone we haven't met, we want to introduce ourselves.
* We want to participate in all the games and enjoy them.
* We use all our good manners at the table and during the party.

* When we leave the party, we want to thank our friend and his parents for a special time.
* Leave them one of your smiles.

**BE ON TIME!**

# Always Be On Time!

Birthday parties are very special events.

We don't want to be late.

Our friend who is celebrating can't wait for the fun to begin.

His parents have been blowing balloons, decorating, baking a cake and putting plenty of love and effort into all the preparations.

All we have to do is to be on time and let the fun begin!

We're really celebrating **life** at a birthday party. A birthday is a milestone that we use to measure growth. Every year we grow **bigger** and **older.** We want to grow **better** along the way. Good manners help us to grow. We count birthdays once a year. We count good manners every day, and they count for a lot. The manners we show determine whether we'll be invited again to next year's party.

# Summary

Birthday parties are always special!

We get dressed up. Play good games. Eat special treats.

It's a special time of sharing and celebrating with good friends.

Everyone wants to make it the best birthday celebration ever!

We're part of the party of course, and the best part we can have is to be sure our manners are showing.

Poor manners can spoil the best planned party.

Every guest at a birthday party leaves a gift.

We can also leave the gift of good manners.

Chapter 15
COMMUNITY MANNERS

# Community Manners

We all "belong" to a community that includes those on the other side of town as well as the folks next door.

Community interests effect us all. We use the same roads, stores, library, police and fire department, for example. We share the same services. We benefit or suffer together, depending on community conditions.

It's important to apply the Golden Rule in our communities as well as our homes. Just as healthy bodies need exercise, a healthy community needs citizens who exercise their citizenship. It needs citizens who have eyes to see a need, ears to hear a call for help, feet to rush to help and hands to fill the need.

Fifty percent of all American teenagers volunteer on the average of five hours a week. They contribute heavily to the number of Americans who volunteer $150 billion worth of their time each year.

We all want to **help** our community rather than **hurt** it. It hurts, for example, when someone litters or commits a crime. It helps when we practice good manners for the good of all and show respect for our environment and our community.

In a sense, life doesn't begin until we get out of the grandstand and get into the game.

**Life is a lot like tennis —
The one who can serve the best
seldom loses.**

Community manners begin in our own neighborhood.

The dictionary says a neighbor is someone who lives close by.

The Bible says a neighbor is anyone in need.

Being a good neighbor requires minding our own business and not our neighbors'. There are times, however, when our neighbor's business becomes our own if it involves a need we can fill.

***If a neighbor is sick and unable to prepare a meal, we can take them one.***

When neighbors are temporarily unable to perform normal household chores, we can help.

Community manners recognize needs around us greater than our own and then serves them.

**The opportunities to help others are limited only by our willingness to serve.**

**Opportunities include:**

★Running errands for a shut-in
★Supplying transportation
★Visiting nursing homes
★Reading to the blind
★Encouraging someone who's "down"
★And something as simple as sharing a smile and a laugh

---

***The best exercise for strenghtening the heart is reaching down and lifting people up.***

---

It's nice to see that good community manners live on a two-way street. As citizens show their concern for one another, everyone benefits. Our neighborhood becomes a better place with each act of kindness.

★ ★ ★ ★ ★ ★ ★ ★ ★ ★ ★ ★ ★ ★

**If you think the world is cold,
make it your business to build fires.**

There are several organizations and institutions in our community that can't function without volunteers.

**They include:**

★Hospitals
★Churches
★Schools
★Charities of all kinds
★Nursing homes
★Service clubs
★Libraries
★Little League
★Neighborhood watch

Each of us has a special talent to offer our hometown and our neighbors. It's good manners to share our abilities.

★ ★ ★ ★ ★ ★ ★ ★ ★ ★ ★ ★ ★ ★

We all want to be informed about issues and events in our community. Our gardens need attention; so does our community, otherwise weeds will choke out flowers in one and pride of citizenship in the other. Without care, both become jungles.

Nations that are most enduring are those in which citizens have the highest sense of civic responsibility and are involved for the common good.

If eligible, we want to be registered and exercise our vote.

Regardless of age, we want to be involved at the level of our ability.

Being involved is a privilege that only freedom allows.

***"As in all of life, the critical thing is whether we take things for granted or take them with gratitude."***

*G. K. Chesterton*

Every community needs *leaders* as well as volunteers. Obviously, we don't become leaders overnight. It takes time, talent and experience, for example, to become mayor, but every school needs student leaders. Every club needs a president.

Every American president climbed a long leadership ladder before he reached the White House.

A leader has been defined as one who *knows* the way, *shows* the way and *goes* the way. In other words, good leaders inspire and set an example as well as organize and direct.

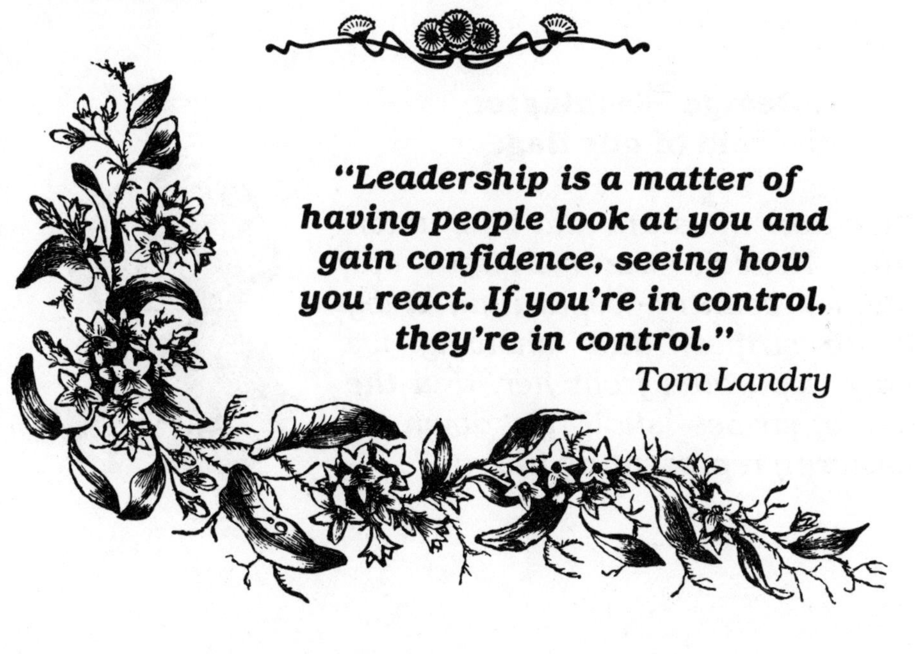

***"Leadership is a matter of having people look at you and gain confidence, seeing how you react. If you're in control, they're in control."***

*Tom Landry*

# Our Flag

Our flag is far more than a colorful piece of cloth. It's a symbol of America's ideals and purpose; an emblem of hope, help, freedom and opportunity.

When we salute our flag, we're reminded that we are **one nation, under God,** made up of millions of individuals from hundreds of other countries. Our flag flies for all of us.

Because it's such an important symbol, we show special respect for our flag. We allow no other flag to fly above it.

**George Washington said of our flag:**

*"We take the stars and blue union from Heaven, the red from our mother country, separating it by white stripes, thus showing we have separated from her, and the white stripes shall go down to posterity representing liberty."*

Our flag is really a symbol of ourselves. It is what we make it.

☆☆☆☆

We inherit it with proud, flying colors. For over 200 years, our people raised it to the highest symbol of freedom and justice in all history.

☆☆☆☆

Our dreams, our faith, our allegiance keep it flying.

☆☆☆☆

Every time we perform an act of kindness for a neighbor, each time we render service to our community, we not only knit the fabric of our society a little tighter, we also strengthen the bond of the stars and stripes.

☆☆☆☆

Our flag will fly in peace and freedom as long as we pull **together** and not pull **apart.**

Today, community is no longer measured by fences, county lines or even oceans. Space shuttles and satellites remind us that the earth has become the ultimate community.

What happens next door and on the next block not only effects us; what happens on the next continent can also effect us.

As a result, we don't want to keep our good manners at home. They need to cross oceans and touch every corner of our world.

*The Family Book of Manners* doesn't presume to be the final word on the subject . . . only a guide. We hope you find it helpful and interesting in your home.

These fifteen chapters don't cover every aspect of etiquette because we've tried to stick to basics. We've concentrated on the life experiences we're most likely to encounter, to emphasize those things that go to the heart of the matter: Courtesy, attitude, behavior, relationships and love.

*The best way to measure our manners is to use the Golden Rule.*

The manners that matter most touch more than our style; they touch our lives.

Hermine Hartley
Al Hartley

***"Dear friends, since God loved us, we also ought to love one another."***
*1 John 4:11*